# HEALTHY HOUSEPLANTS A – Z

# HEALTHY HOUSEPLANTS A – Z

## Anita Guyton

**ISIS**
**LARGE PRINT**
MAINSTREAM SERIES
Oxford, England
Santa Barbara, California

British Library Cataloguing in Publication Data

Guyton, Anita
  Healthy Houseplants A-Z
  I. Indoor plants. Cultivation — Manuals
  I. Title
  653.9'65

ISBN 1-85089-245-8

Phototypeset, printed and bound by
Unwin Brothers Limited, Old Woking, Surrey.
Cover designed by CGS Studios, Cheltenham.

# CONTENTS

To my dearest parents.

Most people think
they have the best in the world,
but I know it.

# CHAPTER ONE

# Suitable plants for your home

Indoor plants are a pleasure in which we can all indulge throughout the year. In the autumn and winter, when everything outside is slowly dying or dead, and we have only the cold days and long dark evenings to look forward to, we naturally clamour for flowering pot-plants in the bright colours reminiscent of summer — the brilliant pinks and reds, the yellows as welcoming as the warm sun, the oranges which delight us, and even the whites which are often more sweetly-scented than those with more vivid hues.

When the spring and summer seasons come round, those people who live in high-rise flats, with not even a few square feet of balcony to call their own, almost certainly miss a garden, and so they do the next best thing. They turn their homes into gardens of dreams, and often the results are wonderfully attractive! I can understand, for my home is always just such a place to me, and yet I am fortunate enough to have an outside garden too.

A lot of money can be thrown down the drain if, when buying a plant, you do not consider conditions prevailing in your home, and these include lighting. If you ignore this important point, and buy a plant simply because you like the look of it, your efforts will almost certainly be doomed to failure from the beginning. Even if the plant does not expire, it will probably never become the handsome specimen you hoped to see.

The following suggestions are guidelines only, because in the pages ahead I have explained each specimen's needs as fully as I can. Let us start with a very light yet sunless room. This will suit many varying plants like the climbing Kangaroo Vine (*Cissus antarctica*), the two-toned Devil's Ivy (*Scindapsus aureus*), the Grape Ivy (*Rhoicissus rhomboidea*) and the quaint and trailing Creeping Fig (*Ficus pumila*), which, by the way, does not resemble its relation the Rubber Plant in any way at all. If these are not exactly your cup of tea, what about the handsome Swiss Cheese Plant (*Monstera*) which can become a real monster, or the slow-growing Dwarf Palm (*Chamaedorea elegans*), the flowering Cineraria (*Senecio*), and the more difficult and striped Zebra (*Aphelandra*)?

Rooms which receive only a little mild sunshine, in the afternoon perhaps, when the summer sun is not too fierce, will suit the variegated Spider Plant (*Chlorophytum*), the Mother-in-law's Tongue (*Sansevieria*), and gay Slipper Flower (*Calceolaria*) and the Cordyline, with its exotic and delicate leaf markings. The sills of south- or west-facing windows can get piping hot, and for many plants could prove a certain death sentence. The desert prickly cacti, however, are made of sterner stuff, and as long as they are not placed too close to the glass, they will usually thrive. Mine certainly do. A while ago my husband came home with a little gift, an Opuntia — one of those flattened oval-shaped cacti. As the greenhouse was choc-a-bloc, my new acquisition was duly placed in a room like this, and it is flourishing — it is now double its original size, and still going strong. With it, although they are several feet away, are some Coleus — the brilliant light does wonders for their colours; then there is the Shrimp (*Beloperone guttata*) and the Chinese Rose (*Hibiscus*), both of which flower more readily in such conditions.

Cool and shaded surroundings are better for the Marantas, the Ivies (*Hederas*), the all-green Sweetheart Vine (*Philodendron scandens*), numerous ferns, and the Primulas, Cape Heather (*Erica*), and the trailing Fuchsias.

Only some foliage plants can cope with the gas fumes from fires and cookers, and these are usually the thick-leaved types such as the Rubber Plant (*Ficus*). Only a few bloomers are immune, for example the Busy Lizzie (*Impatiens*), and African Hemp (*Sparmannia africana*).

Lots of do's and don't's, aren't there? But if you try to force, say, a cactus to live in a shaded corner, or the Creeping Fig (*Ficus pumila*) to reside in a sunny spot, you will be more busy than your local undertaker — doing exactly the same job! Next time you visit the florists, or get a sudden urge to buy a specimen you see, check up on its likes and dislikes first — you can carry this book in your pocket — it could make all the difference!

# CHAPTER
# TWO

# Understanding watering

Water is as essential to plants as food is to people, and the same principles of intake apply to our greenery as to our own bodies. Indoor plants, which live in a very artificial environment, have to depend, not on nature's usually well-balanced diet, but on our own ministrations.

Watering is obviously necessary although constantly drowning the roots, as many people do, will almost always kill plants more quickly than under-watering them (though I do not include here the aquatic plants which often thrive partially immersed in water). Once you realise a particular specimen's needs, the art of watering is not difficult, and yet it is surprising how so many plants fail as a result of too much kindness (excessive watering) which is really a total lack of understanding. This chapter will, I hope, help to overcome such problems, because not only do I want you to enjoy this thrilling world with me, but also I do not want your plants to suffer unduly either! So, how do you go about gauging a plant's liquid requirements? Experience is the finest teacher, and one can quickly begin to understand and sense an individual's needs. The process can, however, prove to be an expensive lesson, so always try, if you can, to read first about the varieties you already have, the circumstances in which they grow in the wild, how much water they require and when. Their needs will vary, and will depend on the time of year and the conditions under which they live. If you are thinking of purchasing a plant for the first time, try to choose those fairly easy varieties, such as the Busy Lizzie (*Impatiens*), the Flame Nettle (*Coleus*), and the ever popular Spider Plant (*Chlorophytum*), none of which are demanding.

The tell-tale signs — and here is where we get to the real root of the matter, pardon the pun — can invariably be found in the compost, and this should always be your guide. As a general rule-of-root, the compost is best left unwatered until the top inch or so of soil has become dry to the touch. Then water the individuals thoroughly. This applies particularly in the summer months when they should be soaked, but always allow the excess water to drain away completely before returning them to their living quarters. Then the treatment should be repeated only when the compost looks dry again. Constant soakings before the plant has had an opportunity to absorb all the moisture will probably cause the roots to rot. The trouble may come before you realise that something is wrong, and then, perhaps, it will be too late. (This rule does not apply to that minority of plants like the Creeping Fig (*Ficus pumila*) for example, which must never be allowed to dry out completely.)

Lots of people expect the foliage to indicate a lack of water, but it does not always tell the true story. Very thick-leaved varieties like the Swiss Cheese Plant (*Monstera*) and the Rubber Plant (*Ficus*) originally lived in very hot climates, and nature endowed them with some means of protection to ensure their survival. Their smooth rubbery foliage — and remember, all plants breathe through their leaves — allows only the minimum amount of moisture to be lost into the atmosphere. Types like these do not require such frequent watering as do the very thin-leaved varieties with fine hairy or velvety foliage, like the Pickaback Plant (*Tolmiea menziesii*) and Velvet Plant (*Gynura*). With plants like these, flagging foliage is a good guide, for their leaves cannot hold moisture for long, and they droop fairly quickly if there is a shortage of moisture.

More water, more frequently, will be needed during the growing period, when plenty of new leaves and flowers are appearing, and this is generally from mid-spring through to late summer. But always, always, test the compost first! During the late autumn and winter however, most plants — except those favourites, the winter bloomers — will be in a state of semi-hibernation, and apart from the odd new leaf here and there, they will not make any noticeable top-growth at all. During this time, you must never try to force them to grow by feeding them fertilisers, because they need the rest to prepare themselves for the following year. On the whole, they are best kept on the dry side, with only the very occasional light drink to keep them going.

Room temperatures in the winter months vary from home to home, and you must take this into account when watering. Plants growing in constantly warm rooms of 70°F (21°C) or so will require more water than those kept in very cool conditions, and yet they will still not want as much as during the hotter season. This is where you will have to judge for yourself, and this is where that most valuable of assets — experience — rears its useful head again!

There are some helpful little tips born of other people's experience, which are really worth their weight in gold, and here is one of them. Use only tepid or luke-warm water as water straight from the tap is frequently far too cold, and this can, and often does, chill the roots. It is far better either to stand a container of water in the room for twenty-four hours before using it, when it will be the same temperature as the plants, or, if you are in a hurry, add enough warm water to take the chill off.

Rain is their natural refreshment, and it should never be wasted. From my own experience, I know that all plants grow far better when fed this heaven-sent liquid. So, next time there is a storm arm yourself with as many bowls and buckets as you can. You may look a bit crazy dashing outside, but you can always say that you are a rain-worshipper — which, in a way, you are! Most certainly some members of your indoor collection are, particularly the African Violet (*Saintpaulia*), the Pickaback Plant (*Tolmiea*), the Azalea and Cyclamen, the Heather (*Erica*), and even the tough-looking Hydrangea. These are positively allergic to very hard tap-water. If their need for soft water is not satisfied, their foliage will turn a sickly-looking yellow. So even if you cannot collect enough rainwater for the whole family, always keep some aside for the more susceptible lime-hating varieties.

With a topic such as watering, it is extremely difficult to state precise quantities, and whenever I am asked questions on this rather delicate subject I always say what I have said here — if ever you are in doubt about using the watering-can, do not! Remember this useful tip because it will save you a lot of disappointments, and an even greater amount of money, too!

# CHAPTER
# THREE

# Holiday watering problems solved

Going on holiday is always thrilling and yet your fun may be spoiled if you are constantly worrying about your plants at home. Plant-lovers who have just a few specimens should not find lodging them out with a friend or neighbour too difficult. But coping with a large number could prove a headache if you are not quite sure what to do. For one thing, you cannot deposit umpteen plants on a friend's doorstep and expect all your specimens to be afforded the best accommodation. Not only that, but uprooting plants from their familiar surroundings is always very unsatisfactory.

The best solution is to find a kindly person who will be prepared to help. Always try to find a nature-lover, who preferably has some experience with indoor varieties; they really are worth their weight in gold on such an occasion! We would not dream of putting an inexperienced person in charge of a child on holiday, and your plants need sympathy and care, for they are living things too! People who keep plants do so because they have a love for them, and this one cannot have unless one understands them. With such a person there is far less chance of an accident like over-watering happening.

Once you have found such a gem, be kind to her, yourself and your plants, by leaving clearly written and concise instructions concerning each individual left in her care. One of the most certain and efficient ways is to attach a numbered label to each specimen, referring only to this number on your list of instructions. This will ensure that there will be no mix-up between, say, a Dieffenbachia and a Dracaena, and will guarantee that the Swiss Cheese (*Monstera*) will be cared for in the lounge and not the larder!

It all sounds fine, but, of course, there may be a fly in the ointment! Finding anyone at all, in the height of the holiday period, is often difficult, so your arrangements may have to be a solo effort. This is best put into operation just before you actually get in the car and drive away, so always allow yourself a good hour, maybe more, depending on the number of plants you have. Move all your varieties, and I mean those sun-loving ones too, well into the centre of the room, particularly if it is facing south or west. This will prevent any specimens becoming scorched or burned, even if there is a heatwave.

Then remove all the buds and flowers from such free-bloomers as the Busy Lizzie (*Impatiens*), and the African Violet (*Saintpaulia*). This sounds drastic and unnecessary, but the next watering will be the last your plants will receive for a week or two, and this limited moisture is best reserved for the roots and foliage. Even if you did leave the blooms, their beauty would all be wasted, and just imagine the dazzling sight which will greet you on your return! Now give them a thorough soaking, and I really do mean a drenching until the compost is completely saturated, but do not let the plant sit in a trayful of excess water which has drained from the pot, unless the particular

9

variety is one of the aquatic types such as the Umbrella Plant (*Cyperus*), which actually benefits from such treatment.

Have ready some well-washed transparent jars, or some *clear* polythene bags, and cover each plant with one or the other, and, in the case of polythene, securely fasten the open end around the pot so that no moisture can escape. All of your "tiddlers-to-middlers" should now look as if they are growing in their own miniature greenhouses! Finding a transparent bag to fit the bigger plants can sometimes be difficult, and you must cover the compost itself with polythene to prevent any water evaporation. Once this is done efficiently, and no compost is left exposed, your plants should survive the two-week gap, even if on your return they are flagging a little. Hanging baskets, window boxes, indoor troughs and tubs, all can be treated in the same way, once they are removed from their normal sites into a cooler and more sheltered spot.

The extremely efficient watering devices now on the market are marvellous for the odd few pots, but using them on a larger scale to cope with lots of plants is an extremely costly business. You can, however, make your own automatic watering appliance and this requires no skills in carpentry or anything like that. All you need is plenty of wool cut into lengths which will depend on the height of your flower pots and how you arrange the set-up (or you can use very fine plastic tubing). One or two strands are threaded through the bottom of each pot, allowing a foot or more to hang free. You then place your plants on a support, a plate-rack or something similar, and this is placed across the top of a bucket or the bath which has been partly filled with water. The last inch or two of the tails are then dropped into the water, and as long as there are no chinks of bends in your "feeding tube", it should draw up the necessary moisture quite freely.

This is a worthwhile method, but one which should be put into operation a week beforehand, to ensure that all is working well by the time you leave.

# CHAPTER
# FOUR

# Temperatures

Strangely enough, many of our tropical houseplants do not like the heat one little bit, in spite of the fact that they originated in far hotter climates than our own. This factor also applies in the colder months, for although they require a certain temperature to survive, it is nothing like as high as one would suppose. Indeed, heat levels which we consider just comfortable, in the region of 70°F (21°C), are excessive for many varieties, particularly the flowering pot-plants, and most indoor plants are much happier in slightly cooler surroundings.

However, it is not only constant highs which affect them adversely. More frequently it is other contributing factors, such as continual fluctuations in temperature, which eventually cause the plants to give up. In the average home, for instance, the central heating is on full blast in the mornings and evenings, whilst during the day and throughout the night, temperatures drop maybe ten degrees or more. This produces an awful shock to the green residents' systems, as you can well imagine. Even the patchy warmth of coal and electric fires will affect the plants in the same way, so what can you do? You can control the temperatures more accurately, so that you reduce the difference between your highest and lowest readings. This will help enormously, but if it is impractical

12

the alternative is to select a cooler, but not cold, room in which to display your plants. If you decide on this course, and if the change-over is made only gradually, they should not suffer too much.

Houseplants which live indoors on window sills are always very vulnerable because they have to contend with the cold conditions outside, particularly at night, when the curtains are drawn across them, and they are cut off from the rest of the warm room. Unless some protection is provided, or they are moved — preferably well away from the window-glass — they will not escape frost.

Whilst talking about home comforts generally, I would like to say something about draughts, which can play real havoc with our specimens. Never under-estimate these seemingly harmless flows, because whether the weather is hot or cold they will almost certainly take their toll. Beware of all doors, and ill-fitting windows, when it comes to finding a home for that new acquisition.

# CHAPTER
# FIVE

# Humidity

Almost all the beautiful ornamental foliage plants, and many of the plain green varieties, too still live in, or at some time came from, countries which are very hot. At first you may wonder how the plant-life of these countries is not adversely affected by the extreme conditions, but there are very good reasons for their apparent immunity! In the tropical rain forests, for instance, the tree-growth is so intense that the plants receive ample protection from the sun from the umbrella above. But, much more important, these high temperatures are combined with an extremely moist atmosphere. Consequently, if we introduce one of these plants into the rather dry conditions of so many of our homes, it may gradually turn brown and even die. If we can provide the humidity which is missing from these dry homes, not only will the foliage of such beauties as the Croton (*Codiaeum*), the Zebra Plant (*Aphelandra*), and the Rabbits' Tracks (*Maranta*) remain fresh and unmarked, but those varieties which can well withstand ordinary room conditions, will respond even better.

There are several efficient ways of providing your plants with that essential damp air without causing any discomfort or inconvenience to yourself. The first method is the easiest, especially for those who do not have time to make a daily check to ensure that the water has not been completely absorbed and dispersed into the atmosphere. It is also especially suited to those individually potted plants which are displayed together in a trough or indoor window-box. Coarse sand or gravel should be used to cover the base of your holder, to a depth of about four inches, but this will depend on how deep or shallow your container is. Now add sufficient water to cover the container floor, but do not allow the water to reach the top of your floor covering. If it does, the base of your plants will be constantly immersed in the water, which could lead to serious troubles such as root rot. Your potted specimens can then be returned to their newly-furnished home, and if you leave a gap of about half an inch or so between each of the pots, it will allow a free-flow of humidity to rise and envelop the foliage and blooms.

Some prefer such plant displays to look as if they have been planted out, and this is quite effective. Use moist sand to place on the holder floor, and position your specimens in the same way as before. Then pack some well-moistened sphagnum moss or peat around the sides of all the pots. Both may be purchased quite cheaply by the bag from florists, nurseries and some department stores. With the rims of your pots now hidden from view, your arrangement will look more like a small indoor garden.

Solitary specimens may be treated in the same way, if a second but larger container is available, into which the potted plant is placed, and then the gap between the walls is filled with peat or sphagnum moss. One important factor has to be borne in mind. Whichever materials you use, sphagnum moss, peat, sand or gravel, all these must be kept well-sprayed or topped-up, before they dry out. If they do, the object of the exercise will be completely defeated, because where there is no liquid there is naturally no humidity either!

Many smooth-leaved varieties, like the Aralia (*Fatsia japonica*), the Spider (*Chlorophytum*) and the Dumb Cane (*Dieffenbachia*), should be sprayed frequently, not only to keep the foliage free from dust, which is essential if you want to keep your plants healthy, but also to imitate nature. In the wild the rain or dew falls on the foliage, helping to keep the humidity level constant. I have often placed my indoor varieties in the bath, and given them a light and tepid shower, but an old perfume spray is fine for the occasional specimen.

This treatment should never, never be used on hairy-leaved types such as the African Violet. It causes the leaves to rot, and the trouble can spread to the heart of the plant itself.

# CHAPTER
# SIX

# Sterilising composts

Those with a substantial plant collection will almost certainly prefer to mix their own composts in bulk, and it will prove a far less expensive proposition than buying the ready-mixed proprietary brands. However, these pre-packed standard composts are sterilised, which is more than can be said of the loams and leafmoulds you will be using. So, before putting your home blend into use, you must sterilise the ingredients. Otherwise, those bugs and organisms which are already ensconced will have a real breeding day, devouring your innocent plants into the bargain!

Although there are many methods, I have tried here to detail only those which are suitable for the home grower. One way is to use boiling water. Shallow trays are required, into which some of your home mix is placed. Boiling water is then poured over the compost, and some pieces of sacking are then put over the tops to help retain as much heat as possible, for as long as possible. Wait until the now soggy mixture is cold before draining off the water, and only when the mixture is dry and crumbly to the touch should it be used for potting.

Alternatively, the desired temperature of 190°–200°F

(88°–93°C) can be achieved in your oven, but the compost must be wet before it is roasted at the required temperature. An old saucepan with a close-fitting lid will serve your purpose well, but do not leave it much longer, or much less, than thirty minutes. After that time few microbes will remain, and the compost will not have become baked, which would render the mixture useless. Always wait until it has completely cooled before using it, or you may blame me for a few scalded fingers!

There is also a range of chemicals, some of which may be purchased by the amateur horticulturist, which will do the same job. This involves the application of dry powders such as metham sodium, formaldehyde, and dithane, all of which are simple to use and effective. However, the instructions on the packets must be carried out to the letter.

# CHAPTER
# SEVEN

# Pests and diseases

Pests can cause havoc to your plants if allowed to run amok! So you must always keep a watchful eye, particularly in the warmer months when the air is extra dry. A daily inspection of each specimen is all that is necessary, but make it a thorough one, not forgetting to examine those favourite and secluded corners such as in between leaf axils, behind stems and on the undersides of leaves.

Sickly and under-par plants and vulnerable young cuttings are always the first to be attacked. The old saying "prevention is better than cure" is particularly pertinent, for the keeping of healthy and strong specimens is in itself a deterrent to these munching marauders! Frequent sprinkling with tepid water also serves a dual purpose for not only does it envelop plants with the humidity they require, but it also acts as an effective pest repellent. (For the various methods involved, turn to pages 14–15.)

Even the most conscientious growers have minor invasions at times, and it is always as well to keep a general insecticide such as Malathion or Derris at hand. However, it is always good to know one's opponents, so here are a few ways of recognising and dealing with the most likely ones, and some common diseases as well.

PESTS

**Aphids (Greenfly, etc.):** Small groups of flies which feed on the sap, causing distortion of the leaves and a general weakening of the affected plant. *Treatment*: Malathion or Derris or Nicotine spray.

**Leaf Miner:** Tunnelling larvae which live in the leaves, and feed on the sap of the leaves. *Treatment*: B.H.C. aerosol.

**Mealy Bug:** Mites are covered with a white and waxy coating, causing leaf loss and a general weakening of the whole plant. *Treatment*: Malathion or Nicotine spray. A light attack can be dealt with by dipping a fine cotton-wool-covered stick into a solution of methylated spirits, and picking off the offenders.

**Red Spider:** A very small but visible spider, which sucks the sap of the leaves, causing distortion and discolouration. Often a fine cotton-wool webbing can be seen. *Treatment*: Malathion or Derris.

**Scale Insects:** Brown, hard-shelled and scabby-looking mites which leave a sticky deposit. *Treatment*: Remove them with a fine stick of cotton-wool, dipped in methylated spirits.

**Thrips:** Small yellowish or brownish winged insects, which suck the sap causing distortion of the leaves. *Treatment*: Malathion or Nicotine spray.

**Vine Weevil:** Grubs which feed on the roots, causing severe wilting. *Treatment*: Add B.H.C. solution to compost as directed on bottle.

**White Fly:** A tiny white fly. The larvae suck the sap, and leave a sticky deposit behind them. *Treatment*: Derris or Malathion.

## DISEASES

**Downy Mildew:** A greyish mould-type growth. *Treatment*: Dithane dust.

**Mildew:** Whitish powder on stems and leaves. *Treatment*: Karathene spray.

**Root Rot:** Roots become soft and pulpy. *Treatment*: Only rarely can it be dealt with successfully. Cut away infected parts with a clean knife. Allow cut to dry, then dust with charcoal or a fungicide such as Captan. Re-pot in a quick-draining compost. Make sure the pot has ample drainage holes, and only water in very small amounts. If plant survives, make sure over-watering never occurs.

**Stem Rot:** Stems become soft and pulpy. *Treatment*: Do not water until compost is completely dry, and then resume in greatly reduced quantities. Keep plant warm and in a well-ventilated room.

# CHAPTER
# EIGHT

# Talking about propagating

One of the most thrilling times for all keen gardeners is the spring. Then, not only does one look forward to the growing months ahead — which in themselves are exciting enough — but it is the ideal time to increase your stock of most varieties, and there are so many interesting ways in which to do it!

Rearing a Begonia from a solitary leaf is something of a miracle when you think about it, and seeing the tiny new plants appearing always produces in me that wonderful tingling sensation which comes from a real thrill! No doubt some of you will be very familiar with seed propagation, whilst others will find more joy in rooting offsets or stem cuttings. Whatever your pleasure, the marvellous thing is that people like you and me never lose that feeling of achievement when seeing the new stem and leaf rear its head! I still experience this enthusiasm when propagating all types, but unfortunately I am not always able to devote as much time to it as I would like.

Such basic instincts to grow things are in most of us, and whether it is grain, vegetables or houseplants is not that important. Above all, one is doing something which one enjoys, and one's happiness will almost inevitably be conveyed to all those around. Not long ago I was over the moon about a succulent which I had been given, a *Kalanchoe*, which is a vigorous grower from Madagascar. Numerous tiny plantlets had formed along the edges of the long-toothed leaves, and with their minute roots already on, were falling and settling themselves in the compost below. I had seen it before, but it was wonderful to see the way in which nature has endowed this plant to reproduce and so ensure the continuation of its species.

Before I deal with ways of propagating your plants I would like to emphasise a couple of important points. Make sure that your tools, knife, scissors, compost and pot are all quite clean, otherwise you will be unwittingly encouraging bothers, and reducing your chances of success. Another cause of failure is the inclination to over-water. So, if you do not want to rot all your beginners before they establish proper contact with Mother Earth, keep the compost no more than moist.

Now let us deal with the various methods involved.

*Seeds*

Seeds are by far the cheapest way of producing plants in any quantities, and a packet of Busy Lizzie (*Impatiens*) or Coleus should produce far more than you can cope with, unless you intend to use them in profusion in garden borders, window-boxes, and tubs! If you do not want to do that, rear them and then give them away to friends and neighbours throughout the year or use them as Christmas presents! However, perhaps the best answer is to join a local gardening club. If there is not one in your area, simply form your own little society with friends. Then your members can bring along their unwanted varieties, and all can enjoy a "swop-shop spree"!

Any clean shallow container may be used for germinating seeds, as long as there is ample drainage, and plastic seed trays may be purchased fairly cheaply from most gardening centres and department stores. These should be filled to within an inch of the top with one of the specially prepared mixtures, such as John Innes seed compost or J.I.P. No. 1, and then sprayed finely with water just to moisten it. Very fine seeds, like pin-heads, can just be eased in with a finger, and require no top-covering of compost, but the slightly larger ones need to be sown with just a light sprinkling on top. Any which are rather hard-shelled, the Silk Oak (*Grevillea robusta*) for example, are best soaked in water first — about twenty-four hours should be sufficient — just to soften them and aid germination. Although a piece of glass has always been the traditional covering for seeds, I always plump for transparent polythene held in position by raffia or a strong elastic band. That way it retains moisture for much longer. A sheet of newspaper placed on the top will ensure that the seeds receive only diffused light, but as soon as the seedlings appear, remove the paper covering immediately. Though the tied-on polythene does help to retain moisture, a daily check must be made to ensure that the compost never becomes absolutely dry.

When the seedlings are large enough to handle they should be pricked out — a thin piece of wood cut at one end into a wedge shape is an effective little tool — and potted individually into very small containers of J.I.P. No. 2.

*Division*

Dividing plants is straightforward enough, as long as the specimens themselves are broken up carefully without

24

causing undue damage to the roots. Over the years, varieties do become rather top heavy, and certain ones may be split up into a number of sections at almost any time of the year. However, there is always a best time, and this is when the plant shows signs of life again after the dormancy period. For various reasons it may not always be possible to do it then, in which case the summer is the next most suitable season, especially for spring-flowering types which should never be divided whilst the buds are either forming or blooming. A few which respond quite well to this form of propagation are the Marantas (Prayer and Fish Bone Plants), the Cyperus (Umbrella Plants), the Aglaonemas (Chinese Evergreens), the Aspidistras, the Anthuriums (Painter's Palette) and many of the ferns. Just remove them from their pots and gently prize the roots apart. Pot up the resultant smaller portions individually, into containers just large enough to house the root-ball nicely. Then leave them well alone until the roots have had a chance to take a grip on themselves, and their new home.

*Runners*

"Runners" is really an inappropriate name when you realise that, once they become independent, they are never more than a foot or so from the parent plant — perhaps "Crawlers" would be better? In their natural habitat, a family of several generations may, perhaps, grow within a radius of a yard or two, for the plantlets form on cords, or stalks, after flowing has ceased, and as they grow they gradually weigh down the supporting cord until the runner reaches ground level. There they put down roots like legs to hold themselves firmly to the ground, whilst nature takes a hand in severing the connecting cord by slowly rotting it away.

Indoors, these plantlets are often left attached, making an attractive display of hanging foliage, and two of the best known varieties for such a show are the Spider (*Chlorophytum*), and the Mother-of-Thousands (*Saxifraga*). I like to see them trailing down, and my own kitchen is far more interesting because of them. My Spider is a young mother of three, whilst the Mother-of-Thousands is certainly living up to its name — it is at present carrying eleven.

Children love to watch for the appearance of these babies, and using them to rear more plants is really child's play! All you need is a small pot containing a standard potting mixture, standing alongside the mother plant. The baby is lifted into the new pot and pinned down to maintain contact with the compost. I frequently use a hairpin when there is nothing more readily available, but a paper clip, straightened out and then bent into a U-shape is just the job. Once the roots have sought sustenance in the soil, the connecting cord may be severed with a pair of scissors.

## Offsets

Offsets are tiny plantlets which form at the base of the adult plant after the flowers have died. Many succulents and most bromeliads reproduce in this fashion, as does the Mother-in-Law's Tongue (*Sansevieria*), the Dumb Cane (*Dieffenbachia*), and the Kaffir Lily (*Clivia miniata*).

There are various schools of thought about when to move them, and so all I will say is that my own practice of lifting them when they become manageable has resulted in some healthy specimens. Some may be levered out with a tiny fork, whilst others will need some encouragement with the help of a knife. Then, like runners, they should be re-potted separately.

*Cuttings*

There are a number of types of cuttings here, and you will probably find the rearing of certain varieties far more difficult than others. Without a propagator, your chances of success will be greatly reduced if you do not cover all your cuttings with pieces of clear polythene, tying it securely round the pot with raffia. This will act as a greenhouse and prevent them from losing all their moisture. Using sand or peat for rooting is fine, but it is meant to be used just for that. Because neither of them contain any nutrients, your cuttings should be re-potted into a more suitable potting compost as soon as they show signs of having taken.

*Leaf cuttings*

If this section does not excite your curiosity, I shall be flabbergasted and very disappointed. The idea of producing numerous baby Begonias from one solitary leaf is incredible in itself, but the way in which it is achieved is really astounding. Many Rex Begonias can be produced in this way, but only the healthiest of leaves should be used.

Several prominent veins on the underside of the leaf are nicked with a sharp and clean razor blade, and then the leaf is laid face upwards on a bed of moist sand or peat. To ensure that the cuts are in close contact with the compost, several pebbles are placed strategically on top to weigh it down. Then the pot is covered, and apart from checking to make sure that the compost stays moist, it should be left entirely alone. Try it, and after many weeks you will be rewarded with tiny plantlets appearing around the base of the treated veins!

Another equally fascinating way involves the leaf, used, this time, in sections. The *Begonia masoniana* (Iron Cross) and the *Peperomia sandersii* are favourite victims. A selected leaf is cut into fair-sized sections and one of the cut parts of each section is dipped into a hormone rooting powder, before being planted, cut downwards. Treat as before, and the little miniatures will soon emerge from around the edges of the old leaf. *Sansevierias* may also be produced in this way, but this is not recommended because the resulting offspring never inherit that familiar yellow edging. *Saintpaulia* (African Violet) cuttings, with some stem attached, frequently root in a glass of water, particularly if the bottom of the stem is kept just above the water level, but those who have little joy will no doubt prefer the more usual way. A leaf is detached with the required inch of stem, by holding it between the thumb and index finger, and twisting it until it gives way. The end should be trimmed, dipped first into water, and then into a hormone rooting powder. Set in some moist peat, so that only the leaf is exposed, and then covered with polythene, the roots will form, and the new growth appear later. They can take their time, so do not get impatient! I have also reared Peperomias in this way, and they do, at least, seem to get a move on!

### Stem cuttings

Stem cuttings, preferably about two inches long, will sometimes root in water, and, of these, the Coleus, Ivies, Tradescantias, Zebrinas, and Impatiens are the most reliable. Other varieties such as the *Setcreasea* (Purple

Heart), *Gynura, Pilea,* and *Fuchsia* are nearly as accommodating.

The top two or three inches of the existing plant should be cut cleanly across, and after removing the bottom leaves, you should dust the cutting with some hormone rooting powder, and set it in a pot full of moist J.I.P. No. 1. Cover it, place it in a warm, light, yet sunless room, and remove the polythene as soon as the specimen starts to grow.

## *Air-layering*

I must mention an extremely useful treatment known as air-layering, which is a way of improving the appearance of Rubber Plants (*Ficus*) and others. Not normal Rubber Plants, I might add, but those hopeless-looking efforts which, because of age and incorrect treatment, have developed into top-heavy, leggy-looking things, almost without identity except for their few remaining top leaves!

Air-layering is more often used in the spring than at any other time, and is a boon to all indoor gardeners. Lower leaves drop far more frequently during the winter months, leaving plants like the Aralia (*Fatsia japonica*), the Swiss Cheese (*Monstera*), and the Zebra (*Aphelandra*) also looking bare and ungainly. The treatment not only improves the original, but gives you two plants for the price of one, hence my reason for including it in this chapter. Any varieties with fairly thick or woody stems can be dealt with effectively by making an incision in the main stem, at the height to which you wish to reduce the plant. In other words, if you want your subject shortened by twelve inches, the cut must be made a foot from the top. This cut, about a quarter of an inch deep, and an inch or so in length, is made vertically, and a sliver of wood — a broken-off matchstick will do — inserted to keep the wound open. Using a fine brush, dust inside and around the edges with a hormone rooting powder, and cover with a generous wad of well-moistened sphagnum moss. The whole is then bandaged with polythene which should extend at least two inches above and below the level of the incision and be tied firmly, top and bottom, with raffia or string.

Some varieties take longer to produce roots than others, and one of my older Aphelandras recently took some weeks but after some time you may expect to see roots appearing under the polythene. Check the moss regularly for drying — it must be kept wet throughout — and when those new roots finally appear, remove the polythene, and cut through the stem cleanly just below the roots. Your new and more compact top should be re-potted, moss and all, into a recommended growing medium. But do not worry about your bare-looking bottom stem, for, with normal care, it will soon sprout new growth, and will look as good as new.

An even more drastic-sounding face-lift for the Rubber Plant is this. Cut out your leafless length of trunk, not too near the top, and a little way from the bottom. In the top of the potted stem, make a V-shaped cut, and then shape the base of the detached leafy section into a wedge to fit the V cut. Fit the wedge into the V stump, bind the two firmly to a splint and leave it. It will eventually knit together, resulting in a shorter but more handsome looking specimen. Isn't new life exciting?

# CHAPTER
# NINE

# Moving plants to your new home

Whilst I was in the middle of writing this book, my husband and I suddenly decided to move to a new house. Chaos prevailed for weeks, because large chunks of the day, which I could ill afford away from the book, were taken up with the packing, and the rest of my work as well!

It was not the general household goods which took up my valuable time, it was the problem of securely packing hundreds of plants — giant ones, small ones, long awkward trailing ones, energetic, branching, climbing ones, and the prickly ones. I thought I was never coming to the end of them, for it seemed that the more I wrapped, the more there appeared to be still waiting! Now I feel that a few tips would not go amiss for those who have yet to face the prospect of moving house. I hope they will not only make things much easier, but will save you a lot of heartache, and your plants some heartbreaks — or leaf damage at any rate. Just stacking your plants haphazardly in the boot of your car, or standing them on trays in the removal van, does not offer them sufficient protection, and there are bound to be casualties. Yet, with thought, these can be reduced to a minimum, and this necessitates preparing yourself well ahead of D-day by collecting some solid boxes or tea-chests, and numerous polythene bags of varying sizes.

Many of the hanging varieties, like the Tradescantias, often sustain quite severe injuries, and they also have an annoying habit of getting themselves tangled up — it really is the devil's own job to try and separate their tentacles without breaking them. So deal with them, as I did, by gently gathering up all the trailers into a polythene bag, and tying the open end around the pot. Those gargantuan specimens, the Swiss Cheese (*Monsteras*), Rubber Plants (*Ficus*), and many of the Philodendrons need careful packing, and we transported ours in tea-chests, which are absolutely first-class, even if they do not entirely contain your towering giants. With plenty of newspaper packed between the chest walls and flower pot, sliding is prevented, and any branches or leaves which protrude over the top can be protected first with several sheets of dampened newspaper, and then with some dry ones. Collect several of those extra-large polythene bags used by dry-cleaners. One of these can be gathered up and placed, open-end first, over your specimen's head and drawn down over the box, where it should be firmly tied with string. Now this specimen should remain fresh and unharmed throughout the journey. You may be forced to pack your plants off several days prior to the final move, and then each plant will obviously have to be well watered beforehand. If this can possibly be avoided so much the better, for it is always advisable to water your plants only when they have arrived at their destination. Just imagine how much heavier each plant will be after it has had its fill of water! This puts a great deal of unnecessary strain on the boxes, which almost certainly will increase the chances of a container breaking, and the innocent passengers spilling out! It also makes the whole business of moving a much more back-breaking job than it already is.

Finding positions for individual plants in a new home is not always as easy as it seems. As yet you are not familiar with the house, and do not realise, for instance, how far sun will stretch into a south-east facing room. When I moved, some particularly tall specimens went along a couple of days ahead of me, one being my favourite *Monstera*, and I had given very clear instructions about where it should be put. The removal men placed the Swiss Cheese in the specified room, but just five feet away from the window! There it had received lots of strong summer sun, and as a result one leaf had already started to show signs of scorching. Never having lived in the place I did not realise that the sun came so far into the room, and the removal men did not appreciate the danger!

You can work out which rooms face, say, north or south, and such know-how will be a boon when finding the verdure even a temporary siting. Always make sure that your shade-loving types receive no direct sun as mine did, and remember that a north- or east-facing room will house them nicely. With the sun-lovers, particularly the desert cacti, the brighter southern or western parts are best, although if you are moving during the summer months never place them too close to the window-sill.

The high-growers are fairly heavy, and are not the easiest types to hump around, but with the general bother of positioning furniture, and possibly re-decorating as well they will have to be lugged about on a number of occasions. So please take note of this snippet of advice — although simple, it works well! Once the big plant is unloaded and uncovered at its destination, immediately place it on an upturned rug, dust-sheet, or even a piece of strong sacking.

Then you will be able to whisk it from corner to corner as you please without much trouble. No lifting will be involved, because all you have to do is gently pull the undercloth, and along it will come like some docile pet on a lead!

# CHAPTER
# TEN

# Foliage plants — full light

## Ananas

*Pineapple*

My first real surge of excitement for the *Ananas* group occurred one Christmas after the pineapple fruit had been demolished. The only part remaining was the tufted top, and within a few weeks it was once again a growing plant. Now it stands in my lounge, and is a handsome-looking greyish-green specimen of which I am properly proud! Most people consider the variegated Pineapple, which has green leaves edged with cream, to be more attractive, and to look after it is certainly a very prickly experience if you brush against the sharp teeth on the foliage!

Pineapples need only small quantities of water in the dormancy period, although the amount should be increased in the summer. Originally from tropical America, the first *Ananas* to be grown in Britain was reared in Richmond, and fruited in 1715. They require at least 60°F (15.5°C) in a bright yet sunless spot. Feed them occasionally with a branded houseplant fertiliser, and replace the compost annually with a fresh blend of equal

**Ananas**

parts of leafmould, J.I.P. No. 2, and peat. (For sterilising, see page 18.)

Older plants with ideal growing conditions sometimes bring their rewards by fruiting. The variegated *Ananas* may produce gorgeous bright pink fruit, which later will be covered with minute blue flowers, and these are undoubtedly far more attractive than the less colourful but certainly more appetising fruits of the green *Ananas*. Small plantlets appear later at the base of the mature specimen, but these should be left until they are large enough to be re-potted individually.

# Begonia rex

Including this variety in the bright light category will, without doubt, be frowned upon by many. My object is, however, to ensure that the *Begonia rex* does not get the opposite — a semi-shaded and possibly poorly-lit siting — for this lovely plant deserves what it likes best of all, and that is a well-lit yet sunless position. Full sunshine has a seriously detrimental effect, and really must be guarded against.

Any drops of water accidentally left on the hairy foliage produce horrid brown patches, and greatly mar the otherwise strikingly handsome leaves. These must always be kept free from dust, and a simple but effective method is to clean them carefully with a very soft and dry brush — at the moment I am using my husband's shaving brush.

Begonias are often found to be pot-bound when they are purchased, and if allowed to remain so restricted will never grow as well as they should. So, any time from April to September should see them re-potted into a slightly larger pot, containing a quick-draining mixture of two parts of J.I.P. No. 3, and one part of sphagnum moss.

**Begonia rex**

Poor drainage, over-watering, and an over-damp and cold atmosphere — all will cause problems, the most likely being mildew, but this can be treated effectively with Benlate powder. The improvement of poor conditions, and the provision of a minimum 60°F (15.5°C) will make all the difference.

The plant is named after Michel Bégon, who was not only the Governor of French Canada, but a great patron of botany in the 17th and 18th centuries. It can be found in a multitude of colour variations; some particularly handsome strains are *Begonia rex* Helen Teupel (pink, red and silver), *B.r.* Merry Christmas (deep red, green, pink and silver), *B.r.* Salamander (green and silver), and *B.r.* Heligoland (purple and silver).

Once the foliage has faded completely, and the compost is bone dry, the plant should be left in this state throughout the winter, preferably stored in a warm and dry cupboard until the spring. Then the tubers can be re-potted in a fresh potting compost, and placed in a temperature of at least 70°F (21°C). Any which have started to rot during this resting period must have the affected parts cut away, and the uninfected remains should be dusted with charcoal before planting. Watering can be resumed, starting with only a little at a time.

Once the tubers have produced several leaves they may be slowly acclimatised to lower room temperatures of approximately 60°F (15.5°C), and fed with a houseplant fertiliser. Keeping the plants going from one year to the next is a challenge, which many will find exciting and stimulating!

# Caladium

These aristocratic-looking plants from Brazil should be nicknamed "Temptation", because they are just that to any plant-lover. So finely textured that they are almost transparent, the sheer beauty of their large, arrow-shaped foliage takes your breath away!

The two most popular strains are the *Caladium* Candidum, with its white tissue-like leaves deeply veined with green, and *C.* Lord Derby, the rose-pink leaf surfaces of which are edged with green. Although not strictly foliage plants — for the leaves do fall each autumn — they are far too beautiful to omit.

Caladium

There are complications at almost every stage of their life cycle, and the first of these must be faced as soon as you bring yours home. To keep it flourishing in the four months or so during which it is in leaf requires plenty of patience, a steady 60°–70°F (15.5°–21°C), a reasonably high humidity (see page 17), and the avoidance of direct sunshine and draughts. Ample watering is essential during this time, although the compost must become almost but not completely dry between doses. When the leaves begin to die, the liquid intake should be slowly reduced.

# Ceropegia woodii

*Hearts Entangle, Heart Vine, Chinese Lantern Plant, Rosary Vine*

This is really quite a delightful little plant, and I am only sorry that it is not seen in greater profusion. It has fine reddish-purple trailing threads, which support a number of bluish-grey and heart-shaped leaves with silvery markings. As you can imagine, it makes a pleasing addition to any hanging wall display.

They look extremely delicate, and one might imagine having to mollycoddle them, but being succulents, they are much tougher than they first appear. Continual watering during the winter dormancy-period will inevitably kill them, and although a little more liquid is needed in the summer months, do not overdo it! After all, nature did equip them to live without rain for some time in the wild. Again, as natives of Natal, they immediately conjure up a picture of intense heat, yet the "Hearts Entangle" needs only ordinary room conditions in which to flourish (out of the sun). The winter temperature should never fall below 50°F (10°C), and if, like me, you are a hot-house plant, there will not be much chance of that unless the central heating fails!

This variety grows from a corm, and is basically an annual, but do not lose interest because by the time the old growth has died, the new shoots are starting to sprout. So you could almost call it an evergreen, or to be more specific 'ever-grey'. Spring is always the best time for propagating, and the *Ceropegia woodii* is really child's play. As with ordinary stem cuttings, detach some small pieces of the cotton-like stalks, and root them in J.I.P. No. 2.

Very often they will produce their own second gener-

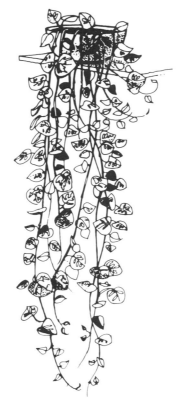

**Ceropegia woodii**

ation if allowed to do so, with the help of a second pot full of compost. The fine attached stalks can be pinned down into the second container, and when they have rooted a short time later, they can be severed from the parent plant.

When concocting new compost for an established specimen, some peat moss may be added to the J.I.P. No. 2, and only a smallish well-crocked pot should be used.

# Chlorophytum comosum

*Spider Plant*

While my husband and I were house-hunting, we came

across a Spider Plant which was looking very sick indeed. There were still traces of its earlier handsome appearance, but it was languishing miserably in a ten-inch pot! Spiders do have thick roots, which in a season become pot-bound quite quickly, yet usually a one-size larger pot is all that is necessary. Unfortunately, this owner had failed to realise that her kindness in giving the roots lots of space had caused her plant almost to die.

These roots are voracious drinkers in the hotter months, and even a daily watering is not always enough. More often than not browning of the leaf-tips will occur, and although this may be due to an over-hot and dry atmosphere, it is much more likely that the plant requires the extra nutriment of a liquid fertiliser. A regular lukewarm spray over the foliage will keep the leaves clean and lush, and it will discourage any pests such as greenfly. However, mild attacks do happen, always, it seems, when you have forgotten to renew your general insecticide spray of Derris or Malathion. Tip the plant upside down — not forgetting

**Chlorophytum comosum**

to hold the compost with one hand — and dunk the leaves in warm, soapy water. This will certainly control them, and will sometimes eliminate them altogether.

The Spider is a real survivor and will grow practically anywhere, although it is most happy when kept in a minimum temperature of 45°F (7°C), with only occasional watering during the winter.

# Codiaeum

## *Croton*

Crotons are not easy plants, but any owner of a greenhouse or conservatory which can provide a steady 60°F (15.5°C) should certainly try them. Those who have not got these facilities, and are still set on owning a Croton, should resist the brilliantly coloured and large-leaved strains, and concentrate on the smaller and more compact growers.

When I lived in a north-facing flat, which did not have as much light as most Crotons require, I still had a fair degree of success with two varieties. These were the Aucuba leaf Croton (*Codiaeum variegatum pictum Aucubae-folium*), and the Miniature Croton (*C.v.p. Punctatum Aureum*), which has long narrow leaves. Although both varieties are speckled with yellow, they are quite unlike each other. They are slightly easier to rear than their relations, and I tried to compensate for the lack of bright light by placing them outside on the window-sill during the spring and summer.

All this family prefer an unfluctuating warmth, and if the temperature falls drastically, they will shed much if not all of their lovely foliage. Ordinary summery days will enhance their vivid colours, but on any really hot days they must be afforded plenty of protection from the sun.

No Croton likes a really dry atmosphere (see pages 14–15), and they are best if sprayed all over with tepid water every day. Their roots must never be saturated, and neither should they be allowed to become quite dry, so a delicate balance between the two extremes has to be maintained.

**Codiaeum**

If something does go wrong in the winter, and they lose their leaves, the stems may be pruned back in the spring, and in a fairly short while they should start to sprout new growth.

These natives of South-East Asia will need to be re-potted annually, the smaller ones in J.I.P. No. 2 and the larger in the No. 3 mixture.

# Coleus

*Flame Nettle, Painted Nettle, Foliage Plant*

The Flame Nettle, especially when reared from seed, is an inexpensive plant to produce, and enormous quantities are used to decorate large borders in public gardens and parks, producing a glorious picture of brilliant yellows, oranges, pinks, reds, mauves and greens.

It comes in a variety of leaf shapes, and has two, three or even four contrasting colours to each leaf. The Foliage Plant, as it is known in America, is also a gorgeous and useful variety to keep indoors, and is not exacting.

This bushy, free-branching breed comes from India, Java and tropical Asia and will grow almost anywhere although it needs plenty of bright light to retain its showy hues. The occasional nipping-out of the top-shoots will keep them thick and compact, but once the old ones start to fade with age it is best to start again with the more brilliant younger ones.

## Coleus

Two- or three-inch long cuttings will root easily in water or sand, and usually thrive when transferred to a crocked pot containing two parts of J.I.P. No. 3 to one part of sand. In the hot weather they have a healthy thirst and sometimes need watering twice a day, but in the colder months far less is required at a time, and only when the compost is completely dry, otherwise the roots will rot. An ordinary room temperature of at least 55°F (13°C) and a weekly feeding in summer will keep them healthy and happy — that is, if aphids or mealy bugs do not get their teeth into them. These pests can be dealt with efficiently with a Malathion spray once they arrive, but can be discouraged from visiting in the first place by increasing the level of humidity (see pages 14–15).

# Dieffenbachia picta

*Leopard Lily, Dumb Cane, Spotted Dieffenbachia*

The Dumb Cane may be simple for some, and awkward for others, but I have always been very lucky with this variety. Even in the days when I was living in a rather dark flat, mine seemed to do quite well, mainly, I think, for three reasons. Firstly, I had central heating which always maintained a steady 65°F (18°C). Secondly, my daily ministrations with a syringe dampened the leaves and kept the surrounding air moist (for humidity see page 17), and thirdly, I tried to make up for the general shortage of light by standing the Leopard Lily outside on the window-sill, weather permitting, and housing it in the lightest spot in the flat. Water can create real problems if it is given too readily. Try to keep the compost almost dry in the winter, and only water it during the growing months when it obviously needs a little refreshment.

Considering that *Dieffenbachias* are variegated, and such varieties are always more delicate than their all-green relations, this is a very tolerant specimen. It is never affected by gas fumes, but it hates draughts, so always

**Dieffenbachia picta**

stand it well away from doors and badly-fitting window frames!

Central and South America is its homeland, and it likes a rich open mixture such as J.I.P. No. 3 with a little extra peat, or a sterilised mixture of equal parts of loam, peat, and leafmould (see page 17). When mature, these plants do produce arum-like flowers in the spring or summer. One which I keep in the house has bloomed each April for the last two years, and although the blooms are not pretty, they certainly add a special interest to this favourite of mine.

# Dizygotheca elegantissima

*False Aralia, Spider Plant*

This is a strange-looking plant, with long, narrow serrated leaves, yet it grows into a striking single specimen, especially if displayed against a lighter background of white, or, even better, gold, I say single specimen because,

**47**

although the almost black foliage looks very effective in a group display, the False Aralia will only remain the beautiful specimen you purchase if it is given perfect care. They do need individual treatment, and this is made much easier when grown by themselves. They are difficult to keep in the home, and anyone with a greenhouse or conservatory and some experience will have a much better chance of success.

**Dizygotheca elegantissima**

The False Aralia was brought to Britain from tropical New Caledonia in 1873, and it requires a minimum winter temperature of 65°F (18°C), a light yet shaded siting, and a pleasantly moist atmosphere (see pages 14–15) at all times. Watering often causes the biggest headaches. If the soil is allowed to remain wet for any length of time, it can result in the foliage dropping, and yet the roots should be well-watered. Water the compost thoroughly when the soil becomes dry and crumbly. Allow any excess moisture to drain away, but remember, never repeat the process until the soil becomes dry again!

Re-pot in early spring in a mixture of equal parts of loam, peat, leafmould, and sand. (Sterilise it beforehand, see page 17.) Any lanky specimen may be pruned right back, whereupon it will sprout new and bushier growth, and you can improve your plant, and propagate another at the same time, by air-layering (see page 29).

## Dracaena sanderiana

This very neat plant, the most elegant of the *Dracaenas*, requires only a little space in which to spread its wavy-edged, eight-inch long leaves, and is an ideal indoor plant for any home with a winter temperature of at least 60°F (15.5°C).

**Dracaena sanderiana**

Being upright, with foliage which rarely exceeds an inch or so in width, it may tend to look a little lanky as it grows taller, particularly if it loses any lower leaves. Then it will probably look better included in a mixed display,

**49**

although the more mature specimens do eventually sprout from the base. However, by maintaining a humid atmosphere (see pages 14–15), and a daily all-over spraying, leaf-loss will be greatly reduced, as will browning of the leaf-tips which often mars the beauty of such foliage plants. My husband bought me one over two years ago, and its leaves are still intact, although I am expecting a few to fall eventually through old age!

I am sure that the secret of success with this specimen lies in correct watering. Confine summer watering to when the compost looks dry, and feed the *Dracaena* only occasionally. Throughout the dormancy period (late autumn and winter) keep it on the dry side. When spraying the foliage, make sure that no water is left in the leaf axils, for it might cause rotting of the joints. The necessary minimum winter warmth should prove fairly easy to maintain in the average house, and then, in April, re-pot in a well-crocked pot of J.I.P. No. 1. Then occasional weak doses of liquid fertiliser will cause no harm.

Named after the founder of the famous orchid nurseries of St. Albans and Bruges. Henry Sander, this hardy specimen should always be selected in preference to the often larger but more delicate Dracaenas.

# Ficus benjamina

## *Weeping Fig*

I recently saw a Weeping Fig which must have been all of eight feet tall! If the owners purchased it as a small plant, they have certainly had to wait some time for this lovely specimen to have reached such an imposing height, for although this *Ficus* does not grow very slowly, it is certainly not extremely fast either!

During the growing months, it produces sufficient new growth to encourage one to retain an active interest in its progress, the new young leaves being bright green at first, then becoming darker as they get older. Like most members of this family, it will grow in a semi-shaded spot if it has to, but I have found that plenty of bright protected light and fresh air makes for a far superior plant. My own large ones are in the conservatory, whilst the smaller ones are outside in the garden enjoying the mild days, from April/May to the middle of September, although they are always brought in again in the evenings. Not only does their growth take on a more graceful and natural look, but they always appear much healthier and stronger.

The *Ficus benjamina* is a native of India and Malaya, and can reach heights of over three hundred feet in the wild, but when confined to a pot the growth is limited to

**Ficus benjamina**

a more manageable size — especially if gently pruned each spring. At this time, the old compost should be replaced with fresh J.I.P. No. 3, and a liquid feed may be administered occasionally when watering the compost to keep it just moist. Over-watering can easily occur in the colder months, so let the growing mixture dry out before re-watering in much reduced quantities.

Ordinary room temperatures of at least 60°F (15.5°C) will keep it quite happy, and although some leaves will turn yellow and fall, this is just something to be expected.

# Ficus lyrata

## Banjo Fig, Fiddle-leaf Fig

The *Ficus* family are so diverse in both leaf-shape and growth that it would have been such a pity to have mentioned only a couple here, and instead I have devoted several pages to this exciting group.

In recent years the human yearning for more living space has produced larger rooms and removed unnecessary walls, so that this large grower, the Banjo Fig, with its large violin-shaped and bright-green leaves, is at last finding a way into our hearts.

In its native tropical Africa, which has a low rainfall, overhead watering is immediately directed by the specially designed foliage straight to the root-ball. Nature's wonderful way of not wasting any precious rain can easily lead to over-watering when growing them indoors. To prevent unnecessary problems like root-rot, during the summer the *Ficus* should be thoroughly soaked and then left to become quite dry before watering again, whilst in the winter the compost is better kept not far from dry. Average room temperatures — and these rarely fall below 50°F

**Ficus lyrata**

(10°C) — suit the Banjo Fig best. The foliage must be kept dust-free, but remembering the dangers of frequent overhead spraying, the cleaning is best done by sponging the leaves individually, with luke-warm water.

Annual re-potting — about April — is essential, using either J.I.P. No. 2 or 3, according to the size of the plant, or if you want to make yours really bolt, try two parts of sterilised leafmould (see page 17), two parts of J.I.P. No. 2, and one part of sand.

# Ficus pumila

*Creeping Fig*

Another member of the *Ficus* family, but so very opposite in both appearance and habit that one would never guess the Creeping Fig was even a distant relation. A natural trailer or climber, it is used in a wide range of mixed displays, and once, when I moved into a new place, I was more than grateful to this small-leaved evergreen.

At the end of my new nineteen-foot lounge was a small electric fire which had been inserted in the wall at eye-level. It was a real eye-sore, and as we had central heating it was of no practical use. I was in a hurry to move in and did not want the messy business of builders pulling it out, and then I had one of my rare brainwaves! I was fortunate enough in already having a fairly well-established Creeping Fig, and after securing a length of light trellis-work over the fire, and extending it from the ceiling to the floor, my Creeping Fig was duly hung in position. I am convinced that it realised it had a practical as well as decorative role to play because it grew and grew and grew, quickly covering its support with a gloriously thick screen of deep green foliage.

**Ficus pumila**

All plants have individual characteristics and part of my success with the *pumila* was due to the fact that I never allowed the soil to become absolutely dry — this is one of the few plants which actually benefit from a constantly damp compost. Away from draughts in a light and sunless room, it thrived in its J.I.P. No. 3, leafmould, and sharp sand. Each spring it was encouraged to branch freely, by pruning the top few inches of winter growth.

Any strong cuttings, by the way, will root easily in water, and in their turn can be potted-up separately, or, if you want a really large and bushy effort, in their first home with the original plant.

# Ficus robusta

## *Indian Rubber Plant*

In past years, all-green Rubber Plants could have been one of several varieties like the *Ficus elastica* or *decora*, but these have, in the main, been superseded by the much hardier *Ficus robusta*. Robust it may be, but it still cannot withstand saturation of the compost which will soon cause the roots to rot, and the lovely deep green foliage to fall, leaving a bare and sorry-looking tree.

If this problem has already arisen, your only chance lies in treating the roots immediately. Gently remove the soggy compost with your fingers, exposing the roots, cut away pappy and infected parts, and dust each cut with charcoal. Then re-pot in a not over-large, but well-crocked pot, in J.I.P. No. 2. It should be safe to water the compost in a few days, and in between future waterings, always wait for the top-soil to dry out!

During the spring and summer, a tall and lanky specimen which has lost many of its lower leaves may be greatly improved by cutting out a few feet of the bare trunk. Now being left with two separate sections — the

**Ficus robusta**

leafy top and the rooted bottom part — make a wedge-shaped cut at the base of the top section, and a V cut in the stump, so that the two can be fitted snugly together. After binding these firmly, a strong cane will be necessary to support the doctored plant. Once the two units have knitted, the binding and cane may be removed, leaving a more compact and leafy specimen.

However, no such operation will be necessary if draughts, very dark corners, over-watering, and cold water are avoided, and a minimum 55°F (13°C) is maintained throughout the year. Although this native of Malaya will grow in a shaded spot, a bright light out of the sun suits it better, as does a relatively small pot, and only when it is root-bound should it be moved into a one-size larger container.

# Grevillea robusta

*Silk Oak, Australian Wattle*

The Silk Oak comes from Australia, and is found growing near the coasts in the bush or rain forests, sometimes reaching tremendous heights of over one hundred feet! When restricted to a pot, the growth cannot reach such tree-like proportions, but after a few years yours may easily grow to five or six feet. Then it will drop some of its lower leaves, and begin to resemble the tree it really is. Cultivated quite extensively in Sri Lanka both for the timber and the shade provided by the wide, silky and fern-like branches, it was named after Sir Charles Greville who, in the 18th century, founded the Horticultural Society of London.

**Grevillea robusta**

Although they come from a very hot climate, they do not demand the intense heat of their homeland — 60°–65°F (15.5°–18°C) will keep them quite happy. Plenty of light with fresh air are essential so advantage should be taken of warm days to put the Silk Oak outside in a shaded spot, where it will benefit enormously! Like many other quick-growers, the Silk Oak thrives when provided with fresh J.I.P. No. 3 compost each spring, and a regular feed with a houseplant fertilser which should be continued until the autumn.

Anyone who has a friend with a mature pod-producing plant should not miss the opportunity of accepting some of the small, ripened black seeds inside. These, when sown in a moist and sandy compost, and covered with polythene, should soon germinate in a warm and dark cupboard — my airing cupboard is always used as an extra propagating box! Once the seedlings appear, remove the cover to give them plenty of light, and when large enough, they should be potted into J.I.P. No. 1.

# Gynura aurantiaca

## *Velvet Plant*

Usually, blossoms on plants kept mainly for their foliage are an extra treat, but in the case of the Velvet Plant there is certainly no bonus about them. You may be fond of all flowers, but please take the advice of someone whose nose knows its job, and remove them as soon as they appear. If you do not, they will most certainly move you out, for they exude such an offensive pong that their only use would be of ridding yourself of unpleasant guests!

However, do not let this disadvantage dissuade you from keeping this otherwise beautiful plant, for its rich, velvety purple and green leaves are a real joy, and very good light always enhances the colours.

**Gynura aurantiaca**

The Velvet Plant is simple to rear from cuttings, for several two- or three-inch top pieces, when dipped in a hormone rooting-powder, will take very easily. Once they are re-potted in J.I.P. No. 1 they will make handsome plants, particularly if the top-shoots are nipped out whilst they are still young. If they are left untended, the plant could become straggly and unattractive.

Being indigenous to Java, they can tolerate and enjoy far more sun than is usual for the large majority of foliage plants, and they also need winter warmth of at least 50°F (10°C), although 60°F (15.5°C) is better. The compost must be allowed to dry out before re-watering, but should never be left dry for any length of time, for they need a damp growing mixture, and plenty of humidity (see pages 14–15). Liquid doses of weak fertiliser will benefit the Velvet Plant enormously, but should be discontinued during the winter months.

# Hedera

Part of the fun in growing Ivies is that you do not have to buy them! You can find so many gorgeous varieties with different markings and leaf-shapes by just keeping your eyes open. Not only are there many strains still growing in the wild, but with relations, friends and acquaintances, you can have a never-ending source of cuttings, which will root easily in water, ready for potting in a mixture of J.I.P. No. 2 and sand.

The first time I realised the appeal of Ivies was when I was young, and my parents had a wonderful gardener, Joe. Being a lover of outdoor plants, he did not go in for houseplants generally, but old Joe did love Ivies, and spent some time constructing a wooden trough on legs, about six feet long. Canes of varying lengths were attached

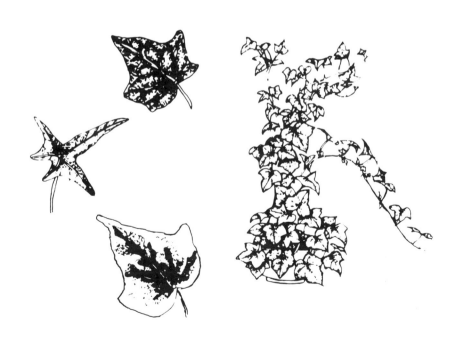

**Hedera**

around the sides, and from the legs cords were attached in a criss-cross fashion. He filled the trough with two-toned and all-green Ivies which he had reared, and it looked absolutely stunning! They were growing exactly as they liked, some up the canes, some climbing over the sides, and still more cascading down the legs and hessian cords. Within a comparatively short time, you could not see the trough for the thick blanket of foliage!

I have found that daily sprinkling of the foliage, and the provision of plenty of fresh air, are the Ivies' two most important requirements and any light summer showers will see me grabbing all the Ivies and putting them outside in the rain. They do not mind waiting an extra day to be watered, especially if they are kept in the cool conditions they favour — 45°–60°F (7°–15.5°C), but during the winter, leave them very much on the dry side.

# Neoregelia carolinae tricolor

This magnificent bromeliad is just one of many epiphytic plants, which attach themselves to trees and rocks for support. Their homeland is in the rain-forests of tropical South America. With only a relatively small root-growth, the brightly coloured leaves grow from a central vase which acts as a cup to collect extra moisture, and even in cultivation this urn must always be kept topped up, with rainwater if you can.

There are various ways in which such plants can be displayed, but if you have sufficient space in a sun-lounge or conservatory, the most impressive spectacle is produced by attaching them with cork bark and fine wire, to a dismembered tree branch. This can be placed across an indoor pool, so that the evaporating water will provide the essential humidity.

**Noeregelia carolinae tricolor**

A moist atmosphere can be easily supplied in a far less exotic fashion, however, (see pages 14–15), and the Neoregelias, which have creamy-pink and green striped foliage, and vivid red rosettes, are also happy in an ordinary pot containing a mixture of leafmould and peat (for sterilising composts see page 17). Such a porous blend should be kept damp, but never soggy, and a controlled temperature of at least 60°F (15.5°C), preferably 70°F (21°C) is essential.

The tiny blue flowers are far from exciting, but they are of some interest as they appear from the rosette. They do not, however, grow far above the water level, and, as with most bromeliads, once the blooms die tiny plantlets form around the base of the adult specimen. These should be left undisturbed until they have developed several leaves, when they can be removed with the aid of a sharp knife and potted in a peat-filled container. Later they can be re-housed separately in a more suitable growing medium.

# Nolina recurvata

Named after P.C. Nolin, a French writer on agriculture in the eighteenth-century, the Nolina was first discovered in South-East Mexico in 1845. Sometimes known under the generic name of "Beaucarnea", this succulent has many popular names such as "Pony Tail", "Elephant Foot" tree, and "Bottle" plant, each one attempting to convey the appearance of this Yucca look-alike. To those with some imagination it can be likened to a cork bottle with a short swollen base, and a long thin neck from which trails masses of tassel-like green foliage which cascade down in a most graceful fashion. Its greyish-brown and deeply wrinkled trunk — hence its close resemblance to an elephant's foot — serves as a natural water reservoir, which enables the plant to withstand intense heat and the prolonged periods of drought in its native habitat. When growing wild in clumps in the desert — and this really is a sight to see — it reaches a height of around thirty feet (nine metres), and produces masses of small, white scented flowers. But even in the confines of a house, height is not much of a problem, for when restricted to a smallish pot it rarely exceeds eight feet (2.4 metres).

As one might expect, the *Nolina* is not generally hardy, but it can be successfully cultivated out-of-doors in temperate areas which are free from frost. As far as plants such as cacti and succulents are concerned, even the seemingly brightest homes usually provide poor and inadequate light. Yet we can do much to alleviate this problem, by placing the "Pony Tail" in a protected, wind-free and sunny spot out-of-doors during the height of the summer. There, it can bask in ample fresh air and sunlight, thus satisfying its need for at least twelve hours of natural light each day, but always return it to a place under cover before there is a frosty nip in the air. Once indoors, select the best position available, preferably on either a southerly- or westerly-facing window-sill, where the night temperature does not fall below 55°F (13°C).

**Nolina recurvata**

One of the biggest difficulties with types like the Nolina is unquestionably that of correct watering. Unfortunately, far too many of us regularly over-water all of our specimens, and such mismanagement kills all but aquatic plants in no time at all. Always allow the Nolina's compost to become absolutely dry to the touch between waterings, and then, having "fed" it, immediately remove any moisture which has drained through and collected in the "splash" tray below. During the resting period between September (autumn) and the end of March (late winter), water must be given even more sparingly. If the specimen suddenly starts to wilt, the leaves curling, yellowing, and falling en masse, one can safely assume that either an inadequate or excessive amount of moisture is the cause. So, remove the plant from its pot, loosen the "soil", and examine the roots. If they appear healthy, and look nice and white, re-pot in fresh compost and water thoroughly. Soft and pappy diseased roots must be cut away, and there is always a good chance that the plant can be saved when only a few roots have been adversely affected. Re-pot in a suitably sized container with ample drainage holes, keeping the growing medium dry until signs of new growth become evident.

Newly-purchased, and freshly-potted established specimens, will not require additional nutrients in the form of liquid fertiliser for at least twelve months, from which time on they can be fed just once a year at the end of April (spring), using a house/indoor plant food. When re-potting mature specimens in spring, to use a quick-draining compost is essential. A blend which I find particularly good is one composed of equal parts of J.I.P. No. 2, peat moss, and either sharp sand or vermiculite granules. To every bucketful of this growing medium add a further two tablespoonfuls of an all-purpose fertiliser, and mix it in thoroughly. The "Elephant Foot" will grow quite happily for a number of years in a comparatively small container.

New plants can be reared by either seed or offsets. Sow seed in a suitable compost with a bottom heat of around 70°F (21°C). When the seedlings are a manageable size, prick them out and re-pot them individually into small well-drained containers, with a mixture of equal parts of J.I.P. No. 1 and sharp sand. By far the easiest means of propagation is to detach the offsets which appear at the base of mature adult plants, and set them in the same compost as that suggested for seedlings. Later, when these young plants have outgrown their "baby" stage, they should be re-potted into a mixture better suited to adult specimens.

# Pandanus

## *Screw Pine*

One has to hunt around for Screw Pines, but they are well worth it. The shortage is due to the plants themselves, which produce plantlets from the base of the adult specimens in only very limited quantities. Any trouble you have in locating one will be amply rewarded as the plant ages and its trunk becomes twisted, like a corkscrew. Looking as beautiful as it does, with its unusual shape, many would think what a marvellous inclusion it would be in a mixed display, but this is just not so.

The *Pandanus* only gives its best when allowed to go it alone. Then the serrated-edged leaves spread out in all their glory. One of the better known, and probably the most suitable, indoor variety is the *Pandanus veitchii*, which has lovely dark green foliage edged with silver, and was named after the famous nineteenth-century nurseryman, Thomas Veitch.

Some natives of South-East Asia use the leaves of the tree-like *Pandanus* types to thatch the roofs of their homes! Many strains also produce edible fruits which taste like an apple, so when I find myself stranded on a desert island I hope to have plenty of these shrubs to house and feed me!

Seeing them growing in the places where they live is a lovely sight, but so are our own potted specimens, if they are well cared for. They hate extremely cold conditions, although a minimum 60°F (15.5°C) in winter is quite adequate. Water the J.I.P. No. 3 compost freely each time

**Pandanus**

it becomes dry, in the summer, but from the autumn onwards they should be kept nearly dry. Older plants will develop aerial roots, and these should be left to grow freely until they are long enough to be directed into the growing medium.

# Philodendron panduraeforme

*Fiddle-leaf Plant, Horsehead Plant*

At first I decided against including the Fiddle-leaf Plant; it is a magnificent climber, but I pondered that perhaps it would be better to deal with a smaller and more compact Philodendron especially as many homes have only limited space. It was not until we visited a couple of friends in their cosy, but not enormous, flat that I changed my mind. There, in the corner of the lounge, was a handsome specimen, which did not take up much floor space, because it was not very wide. It was climbing a moss-covered pole which just touched the ceiling, as did the plant itself.

Standing away from the sun in a light corner, it was the focal point of the room. It had been purchased only two years before as an eighteen-inch baby, and was now looking extremely elegant in all its eight-feet plus, rich green, fiddle-shaped foliage. Growth was now being limited by cutting out the top shoots, which was improving the plant's overall appearance, and each spring most of the old compost was loosened and replaced with a porous mixture of J.I.P. No. 3. with enough peat-mould and peat moss to keep the blend rich and well aerated.

**Philodendron panduraeforme**

It was both inconvenient and difficult to syringe the leaves of such a gargantuan example to keep them moist and dust-free, so instead they were sponged frequently with a soft wet cloth. The aerial roots were directed back into the just moist compost as an added source of sustenance, and this giant benefited enormously during the growing months when it was fed with a houseplant fertiliser.

These plants come from the jungles of South and Central America and naturally enjoy warm surroundings which should never fall below 55°F (13°). They also require humid surroundings throughout the year, see pages 14–15. From April to September a pleasantly damp compost suits them, but for the remainder of the year watering is best kept to a minimum.

# Pilea

Pileas are not difficult to tend as long as you are careful with the watering-can, and they are so varied in their leaf colourings that they make a very delightful picture when grouped together in a shallow container.

A couple of years ago I was so thrilled with these compact little plants that I crocked a porous dish, and planted the silver and green Aluminium Plant (*Pilea cadierei*) and the *P*. Moon Valley, which has lovely bronze-green foliage with lighter-green margins. The *P. involucrata* (often known as *P. spruceana*), with dark green leaves and maroon undersides, came next, and then the Creeping Charlie (*P. nummularifolia*), from the West Indies, which has roundish, light green leaves supported on reddish stems. All of them grew happily in a temperature of 65°F (18°C). Nipping out the growing tips is a necessary operation to keep them bushy and attractive, but I did not waste these young shoots — they were rooted and potted up.

All these Pileas are of the Nettle family. They require a not over-wet yet pleasantly moist compost, which you may mix with equal parts of J.I.P. No. 3 and peat. If you have a little well-rotted and sterilised leafmould (see page 17), that, too, may be included. Keep them well away from

Pilea

the summer sun and draughts, and in a humid atmosphere (see pages 14–15) — mine are resident in the bathroom —and they will thrive and give you no problems at all! Later on, some of the leaves may fall, but when the stems are cut right back they will quickly sprout again.

For something totally different, look out for the *Pilea microphylla*. It is better known as the Artillery or Pistol Plant because of the way the flowers suddenly explode, scattering the pollen inside. The thinly divided foliage can cause it to be mistaken for a fern, and fern lovers will probably like it very much. Unhappily, it is not generally considered the most popular specimen.

# Piper ornatum

A member of the Pepper family, this small climbing houseplant could justifiably be kept in the kitchen. The black and white pepper which is used to garnish food is produced from the fruit and kernel of the *Piper nigrum*, which is a close relation of this extremely decorative specimen. Its heart-shaped and deep green leaves are broken by a network of pinkish-silver veins, so unless you live in the kitchen it would be a pity to hide it there out of sight!

To maintain the lovely vivid hues, a good bright light is necessary, and an unfluctuating temperature which never falls below 60°F (15.5°C) is a must. Sudden and severe variations in room temperature will cause the plant to shed its foliage quickly, but although this specimen is not a suitable choice for a beginner, it certainly does not need an expert's care to keep it colourful, leafy and healthy!

The plant is found growing naturally in Celebes. The aerial roots, which form at the leaf joints, will try to seek out moisture, especially as this *Piper* has a relatively small root growth. At this stage a sphagnum moss covered stick, kept moist, is particularly useful so that the aerial roots can anchor themselves to the moss, in order to draw the extra liquid nutriment. A piece of cork bark is just as good, and often looks more natural. Spraying the bark daily can be combined with a sprinkling of the leaves. This small, fairly slow grower requires only a little space, and being a lover of damp air could be grown in an enclosed display like a terrarium or bottle garden.

**Piper ornatum**

The John Innes No. 1 compost must be renewed every year in early spring, but the *Piper* can be kept in the same-sized pot until the roots become pot-bound. Try not to be too liberal with the watering-can, for it must be remembered that the root growth is not extensive, and will not take kindly to being drowned!

# Pleomele reflexa variegata

Indoor gardeners who enjoy keeping only those house-plants which are considered medium to fairly fast growers, will probably find little to interest them initially in the *Pleomele reflexa variegata*, for this strain is thought by many to be a somewhat slow-growing variety. Yet, even with this slight disadvantage it really is well-worth having, even if only to enjoy the exotic green leaves which are edged with wide bands of gold. Young plants, which remain on the small side for several years, make marvellous additions to any mixed display, particularly within the enclosed conditions of a terrarium where the slightly damp compost, moist atmosphere, and unfluctuating temperature all contribute to provide the near-perfect environment.

A native of Sri Lanka, the Pleomele possesses the enchanting nickname "Song of India", whilst its genetic name is derived from the Greek meaning "full of honey". This no doubt refers to the blooms, yet when cultivated within the artificial confines of the home it is essentially a non-flowering foliage plant.

As this beauty slowly develops a number of leaves will quite naturally fall from the lower part of the plant, giving it a slightly tree-like appearance, but there is no need for concern for there will always be plenty of new leaves to take over.

**Pleomele reflexa variegata**

Being a variegated strain, it obviously requires a bright and sunless position, particularly from late September to April when the days are short, overcast, and often dull. Closely related to the Dracaena family, many of which are succulents, the compost of the "Song of India" is best kept on the dry side until the beginning of spring. Then it will start to sprout new growth. The growing medium of individual potted specimens should be replenished with a fresh supply each year, and a suitable open mixture is composed of six parts of J.I.P. No. 2, one part of J.I.P. No. 3, five parts of peat, and two parts of sand.

# Sansevieria trifasciata laurentii

*Mother-in-law's Tongue, Bowstring Hemp, Snake Plant*

Some people think the Sansevierias are very uninteresting

73

plants, but I cannot agree. In our local hostelry, there are five, each about two feet high, growing in a dark and draughty spot where beer has been poured over them, and cigarette smoke and butts directed their way. After all that abuse, what do they do? They just keep on growing! I was amazed when I discovered that not only are they very rarely watered, but they have never been fed or re-potted in fresh compost in the six years they have been there! Not a good recipe for success, but by some miracle, they look fairly happy with their lot! They really are as tough as old rope, and such resilient plants are more than a little interesting. Imagine how well they could grow if they were treated well!

**Sansevieria trifasciata laurentii**

In West Africa, where these plants come from, the fibre from the leaves is used for making matting, nets and lines, and I can only hope that this practice does not severely threaten this species.

Such a survival story makes it very difficult to stipulate the essential treatment of these plants, so all I can do is to suggest what the Mother-in-law's Tongue most enjoys. It will exist without much trouble in a dingy corner, but it really prefers good light, a minimum winter temperature of 50°F (10°C), and plenty of fresh air. In the colder months, too much water will certainly cause rotting, so leave them fairly thirsty. During the late spring and summer months the amount you give them may be increased with safety, but do not over indulge them! Repot annually in a well-crocked pot containing J.I.P. No. 3, and prevent those larger fellows falling about by selecting one of the heavy clay kind.

Introduced into Europe in 1904, the Sansevieria was named after the eighteenth-century Prince of Sansevero, but I bet he was not anything like as tough as they are!

# Scindapsus

*Money Plant, Devil's Ivy, Golden Pothos*

These plants will not, as one of the popular names suggests, bring riches to their owner, but there is an Indian belief that with one in the home no-one will ever go without.

Even if you do not credit this, can you really afford to be without one? With variegted and heart-shaped leaves, they are pretty climbers to have around, and are often easy to care for, although this does vary according to the different varieties available. One of the hardiest is *Scindapsus aureus*, the green foliage of which is flecked with gold. It needs to be selected carefully because poor lighting conditions often cause the leaves to turn completely green. To avoid this trouble, choose a bright position away from the sun for it.

**Scindapsus**

The other two strains one is most likely to see are the *S.a.* Marble Queen, which is entirely white except for streaks of green, and the *S.a.* Golden Queen, which is mainly yellow. This last is usually considered to be the most beautiful because of the lack of green in the foliage, but it is this shortage of chlorophyll which makes it a difficult subject to rear.

Found in South-East Asia and Australia, they all respond well to a minimum 65°F (18°C), a moist atmosphere (see pages 14–15), a daily sponging of the leaves, and regular feeding in the leaf-producing months. A watering of the compost is needed only when the top-soil becomes dry, and a mixture of equal parts of leafmould and J.I.P. No. 2, with a little sand and peat to make it light and porous, will help to promote good growth. An extra source of nutriment can be provided by a live sphagnum moss covered stick, but this must be sprayed daily with tepid water to keep it moist.

# Tetrapanax papyriferum

*Rice Paper Plant*

The Tetrapanax — better known as the "Rice Paper Plant" — because the pith contained in its thick shoots is slit into sheets, and compressed into Chinese rice paper — is one of the most elegant and handsome of all decorative indoor plants. Undoubtedly, its main features are the impressive fan-shaped, and lobed greyish-green leaves, which can be in excess of twelve inches across, and the undersides of the young leaves which are generally blanketed with a white felt-like covering.

Where they come from in Taiwan and South China, these eye-catching, tree-like shrubs grow in multi-stemmed clumps reaching heights of anything between ten and twenty-five feet, but as pot plants they can be restricted to a more accommodating three to five feet. Yet even these smaller specimens still require fairly spacious surroundings in which to display their graceful spread and splendour, and although considered to be essentially foliage plants, large clusters of small umbells of white flowers may sometimes be seen around and about October.

A member of the Araliaceae family, and the only member of its genus, the Rice Paper Plant likes a daily dose of three to four hours of lightly shaded sunlight, and about twelve hours of natural light — one good reason why I suggest placing them out-of-doors in a suitable situation which offers the necessary bright light, and which is free of wind during the warmer summer months. Unlike some of the more familiar indoor plants, they greatly benefit while soaking up the shaded summer sun, the ideal day temperature being between 68° and 72°F (20°–22°C). However, these plants are "tender" and must be moved under cover if there is danger of the minimum night temperature falling below 45°–55°F (7°–13°C). Watch out for the onset of the first likely frost!

During the generally overcast and dull days of autumn and winter, through to mid-spring, they still require as much full light as possible, and it is this need for it which makes them better suited to greenhouse and conservatory culture. Specimens living within the darker confines of a house should be positioned alongside a large full-length window, preferably one which is devoid of curtains. However, one word of warning! Never position plants too close to the glass, for the frost will "bite" and damage them!

**Tetrapanax papyriferum**

The Rice Paper Plant prefers a nicely moist compost at all times, so watering should be such as to keep the compost pleasantly but just barely damp to the touch, and not in any way saturated. A good porous compost which is sufficiently fertile to satisfy the plant's nutritional needs is also of paramount importance. Tiny plants just out of the seedling stage will do well in J.I.P. No. 1 compost, but when the roots start pushing through the drainage holes between April and late August (the growing period), thus indicating that the roots are pot-bound, immediately re-pot them into slightly larger pots containing the J.I.P. No. 2 mixture. Repeat this practice again the following year, this time using the J.I.P. No. 3 blend.

Fairly mature subjects of three feet high and over need an even richer compost, such as one consisting of two parts of J.I.P. No. 3, one part of peat, and one part of sharp sand, and add two teaspoonfuls of an all-purpose fertiliser to each full bucket of the mixture. The provision of additional nutrients in the form of liquid fertilisers is generally unnecessary with smaller specimens, except those which have been neither top-dressed, nor completely re-potted in fresh compost for more than twelve months. If you have some such unfortunates, then they, like the fairly large ones, may be fed with a diluted liquid fertiliser, twice a year, at the end of April and the beginning of June.

Propagation is in order any time between early spring and late summer, by either seed, stem cuttings, or "suckers" which form at the base of the adult plants. When rearing stem cuttings, cut the stems into two to three inch lengths, dust one end of each with a hormone rooting powder, and insert the powdered tip into a pot containing sharp sand. Provide a bottom heat of between 70° and 75°F (21°–24°C), and the cuttings should root without trouble.

# Tradescantia

*Wandering Jew, Speedy Jenny, Wandering Sailor, Spiderwort*

No-one could fail with these very varied, very easy-to-grow plants. Even those who are usually undertakers with plants, bringing them in, bedding them down, and then carrying them out again, should find that with most Tradescantias their fingers become greener, and hopes of successfully growing something become re-born.

There are many pretty varieties available; one of the best is *T.* Quicksilver, which has silver and green striped foliage. A very fast grower during the summer, it can make a fine bushy hanging specimen from a cutting in a few weeks. With the Wandering Jews — and when treated well, how they wander! — the finest are produced when plenty of healthy one- or two-inch cuttings are planted in the same pot. Once they have grown a little they can be pinned down near the base, and allowed to sprout more shoots.

A well-holed container, filled to within half an inch of the top with a mixture of two parts of J.I.P. No. 2 and half a part of peat will suit most types, and in the summer this compost should be kept damp but never saturated. Throughout the winter it can be kept on the dry side, especially in cool conditions.

A bright position (but out of the summer sun) is necessary, for dingy corners encourage all-green shoots, and if these are allowed to remain they will take over the entire plant. When they appear they must be nipped back to the last variegated leaf joint, and never used to propagate two-toned plants. The only exception is the Golden *Trade-*

**Tradescantia**

*scantia*, which has larger leaves of cream and green, and can live in a slightly shaded spot, but if it is too dark, it will still produce those warning plain-green shoots.

Named after Charles I's gardener, John Tradescant, other attractive ones are the bronze-green and hairy foliaged *T. blossfeldiana*, and the White Velvet (*T. sillamontana*), a fascinating plant cocooned in a thick coat of white hairs, but unfortunately seldom seen.

# Yucca

This very alien-looking plant, with its thick trunk and stiff green leaves, could at first give one a very false impression when considering how to care for it. It certainly looks a fairly difficult variety which might be inclined to be temperamental in its requirements, but nothing could be further from the truth. Indeed those friends of ours who have an unfortunate knack of killing off all but the toughest indoor plants will be particularly interested in the Yucca.

Like the Sansevieria and Aspidistra, this very hardy plant not only survives, but actually seems to tolerate all kinds of abuse, which is to many not just a miracle, but something of a godsend! Their hardiness is undoubtedly due to the fact that the family of Yuccas are borderline succulents — hence the thick and moisture-retaining trunk — and, actually, many strains can be grown outside, even in a snowy and frosty climate such as ours. Although they enjoy a sunny siting, they can also cope when placed in a semishaded spot. Like most succulent plants, they should be watered only when the compost feels dry, but they will not flag if you give them a little too much in one go.

**Yucca**

One very fascinating thing about these natives of South America is the manner by which the continuance of the species is ensured by a certain nightflier, known as the Pronuba moth. The female moth first collects pollen from the blooming Yucca, and in return lays her eggs in the ovary of the flower. Then, only when her "laying-in" time is completed, she climbs to the top of the ovary and deposits the pollen which she collected earlier over the stigma, thus contriving both pollination for the Yucca and procreation for the Pronuba!

However, propagation of Yuccas can be induced more simply (although not as romantically), by removing the rooted "suckers" as they appear, and planting them in small pots containing equal parts of J.I.P. No. 2 and coarse sand.

# CHAPTER
# ELEVEN

# Foliage Plants — light shade

## Adiantum

*Maidenhair Fern*

There are around two hundred species of Adiantum ferns which come from New Zealand, Australia and South America, and they all seem to enjoy the same growing conditions. Their botanical name comes from the Greek word *adiantos*, meaning dry, and refers to the very efficient way water rolls from their fronds; living in the tropical rain forests, as many do, this must be a very useful method of keeping dry!

Their need for high humidity makes them ideal candidates for any terrarium, but those of you who wish to display them as single potted specimens should try to avoid a very hot and dry room, for such an environment will almost certainly kill them. Somewhere in the region of 50°–65°F (10°–18°C) will suit them best, and the bathroom can frequently provide good conditions, especially if the potted plant is placed in a second, larger container, into which moist peat has been packed. I have seen several magnificent ferns growing in that part of the house —

**Adiantum**

ferns which were not only a joy to look at, but which improved the appearance of the bathroom as well. After showering, it is quite easy to remember to give the *Adiantum* an all-over shower too, and this helps to keep ferns in the peak of condition!

Throughout the summer, when the plant is producing plenty of growth, the compost should be kept constantly moist. During the winter months, however, the ferns will be resting, and extra discretion is required to maintain a damp but never saturated moisture level.

Always try to re-pot your Maidenhair Fern in a fresh growing mixture each spring, and for this I use an ordinary potting compost with some additional peat moss. Any over-large specimens can be divided at the same time into smaller sections, or separated into as many individually rooted pieces as the plant allows. These should be potted up separately and immediately bedded in with lukewarm water.

# Aglaonema

## *Chinese Evergreen*

Strangely enough, only one of the many strains of Chinese Evergreen now in general cultivation comes from China. In the main, these beautifully marked foliage plants are found in the tropical rain forests of Malaya and Burma, and on many of the islands of South-East Asia. Although the leaves differ in length according to each variety, they are all somewhat similar to those of the Dieffenbachias.

One of the better known varieties is *A.C. commutatum*, which has vivid light-green and silvery markings on a darker green background, whilst the *A.C. pictum* has much paler leaves of bluish-green tinged with grey. The once very popular *A.C. crispum*, with its dark green and silver foliage, has fallen from favour since the arrival of the *A.C.* Silver Queen (silvery-grey leaves) some years ago.

When it comes to caring for them, they all require approximately the same treatment. Often they are considered fairly difficult plants to keep in the house, but from my experience I cannot agree. Once they are provided with an unfluctuating temperature of between 60° and 70°F (15.5° and 21°C), and kept away from open and gas fires and oil fumes, they should not prove to be too much of a handful! Living, as they do, in monsoon areas, they obviously need plenty of humidity (see pages 14–15), and so give them a daily overhead showering to keep the surrounding air damp, and safely clean the foliage as well. Some leaf-cleaning fluids might damage the rather delicate foliage, and are best avoided.

In the spring-time, any over-large specimens can be divided into smaller sections, and re-potted into a mixture of J.I.P. No. 1 and a little peat moss. Just enough water

**Aglaonema**

to maintain a damp compost, and regular feeding with a houseplant fertiliser, should be continued until the autumn. Then all feeding must be suspended, and the compost preferably kept almost dry until the following spring.

# Araucaria excelsa

The Araucaria excelsa is an extremely handsome indoor tree which closely resembles our traditional Christmas tree, and being a native of the Norfolk Islands, it is commonly referred to by its popular name of "Norfolk Islands Pine". Throughout the colder months it needs only sufficient water to keep the compost damp, whereas during the remainder of the year more frequent watering is necessary to keep the compost moist at all times and thus sustain the growing tree. It is particularly important during the short dull winter days that it is given as much bright light and fresh air as possible, so try to make a point of standing your specimen out of doors on any suitably mild days. During the hotter months it will of course need some protection against the scorching rays of the sun, and will be quite happy in any cool and sunless spot.

**Araucaria excelsa**

Each spring, small young plants should be potted on into one-size larger containers, and as fully grown six feet tall specimens should finish their days in a ten-inch pot. At this time of the year all old existing compost should be replaced with a new blend of four parts of J.I.P. No. 2 and one part of coarse sand, but if it is neither practical nor possible to implement such a suggestion, the only alternative is to top-dress the soil by loosening and removing a few inches of the stale compost, and replacing it with some of the fresh mixture mentioned above.

During the height of the growing period between May and August, feed your Araucaria every fourteen days with a diluted solution of plant fertiliser, but this practice must be discontinued immediately the tree shows signs of "slowing down" in preparation for the winter months ahead.

Although pruning is neither desirable nor necessary under ordinary circumstances rather tall and leggy specimens which are often the result of poor cultural conditions are best pruned back in the spring. This will encourage even and stronger growth.

# Asparagus sprengeri

*Asparagus Fern*

This simple but elegant fern is occasionally referred to by its other popular name of "Emerald Feather", given to it because of the brilliant green of its fine feather-like foliage. A native of Natal, this species is a natural climber believe it or not, but in England it is rarely if ever displayed in this fashion. Instead, it is frequently set in a hanging basket, either by itself or grouped together with other varieties of ferns, and if the cultural conditions are to its liking the arching stems will cascade over the sides, making it an excellent subject for any hanging wall display.

If the roots are allowed to become quite dry at any time of the year, the beautiful green foliage will quickly yellow, and in the event of this happening the discoloured stems should be cut away at the base to make way for new shoots in the spring. The plant requires ample watering during the summer months, and an all-over spraying to keep the soft spiky branches fresh and the compost moist may be necessary as often as twice a day. Naturally, such frequent watering will be unnecessary throughout the cool non-

**Asparagus sprengeri**

growing winter months, but the soil must still be kept evenly moist.

By early spring — from April onwards will do — well-established plants may be re-potted into a nine-inch hanging basket which has been lined with sphagnum moss, and filled to within an inch of the top with J.I.P. No. 2 compost. Alternatively, they can be transferred to five-inch flower pots containing a fresh mixture of two parts of J.I.P. No. 2, and one part of peat. Smaller plants which have been propagated by dividing roots into two or a number of smaller clumps will need much smaller pots, being just large enough comfortably to house the root-ball and compost. Only when the roots become pot-bound should they be transferred into a slightly larger pot.

Ferns, and this strain is no exception, should be kept in

a light yet well-shaded room, from early June to late September. During this time they will benefit from a regular liquid feed, every ten days or so, using a suitable houseplant fertiliser. However, it is imperative to point out that all nutrients must be discontinued from September until the following spring.

# Aspidistra lurida

## Cast Iron Plant, Parlour Palm

The Aspidistra was discovered in 1822 in China, and was extremely popular in Victorian days, when almost everyone owned one. It is often known as the Cast Iron Plant because of its hardiness, and it certainly earned the right to this name when it not only survived but actually flourished in rooms which were often dark and draughty. I am pleased to say that the Aspidistra, like everything else Victorian, is coming back into fashion again.

Unfortunately, although they are undemanding and easy to rear, they are not always available, and established ones can often be quite pricey, because they are slow growers. There are more devious methods of obtaining one, especially if you have a friend who owns a large one. You can casually remark to her that "the Aspidistra can be safely divided in the autumn", and then be there to help! The resultant small sections can be potted up in J.I.P. No. 1, but when it comes to re-potting a large fellow, J.I.P. No. 3 with a little peat or coarse sand, is often used with good results. Confine re-potting to the spring, but make sure that your growing medium is sufficiently porous. If water does not drain through quickly and easily, more peat or sand should be added.

In the summer the roots should be completely saturated,

**Aspidistra lurida**

by immersing the potted plant in a bowl of water for several minutes, but between such soakings the compost must be allowed to dry entirely.

It prefers cool conditions of approximately 55°F (13°C), although it can withstand temperatures as low as 45°F (7°C). The best way to clean the leaves is to use a soft sponge dipped in water. If you use a leaf-cleaning agent first test it on one leaf before using it on the remainder. Aspidistras sometimes react unfavourably to such products, so it is best to play safe.

# Asplenium nidus

*Bird's Nest Fern*

The Asplenium is one of the most beautiful of all ferns, but is bright green and undulating leaves little resemble most people's idea of how a fern should look. The shiny leaves grow from the centre outwards, making the Bird's

Nest Fern lok like a large shuttlecock. They grow high up in the trees in the rain forest of South-East Asia and tropical Australia, and being epiphytes, attach themselves to the trees for support.

Aspleniums have a relatively small root growth, and derive no sustenance from the trees, except from decomposed leaves which provide a rich source of humus. This point is well worth remembering when providing fresh compost for your own specimens. A good mixture composed of J.I.P. compost (number 2 for a medium-sized specimen, number 3 for a large one) and some peat moss makes a rich and porous home-blend. Another first-class growing medium is a mixture of equal parts of coarse sand, leafmould, well-rotted manure and peat, but this is more easily made if you live in the country! (For sterilising composts see page 17.) Like most ferns, the Bird's Nest needs humidity, warmth (60°–65°F/15.5°–18°C), and a pleasantly damp compost — corresponding approximately

**Asplenium nidus**

to the conditions in which it grows in the wild — so give yours these, and it should flourish.

This is *not* a difficult fern to keep, but problems may arise — brown marks on the foliage, for example. The fault here is likely to be either too low a temperature and a constantly soggy compost, or far too hot and dry an atmosphere. So, try to keep the balance, spray the leaves and feed the compost with a branded houseplant fertiliser during the winter months.

The best way of propagating the Asplenium indoors is to split it into smaller units by division. Sowing the spores which form on the undersides of the foliage of adult specimens is a more difficult task, and although it is certainly worth trying if you have a propagating box, the success rate is very low.

# Banana

## *Musa*

The Banana plant, a perennial, is essentially a tropical variety cultivated for its fruit, yet many strains may also be reared as indoor ornamental foliage plants, which in some instances even bear fruit as well!

The smaller strains, such as the *Musa cavendishii* which reaches a height of some six feet, the *M. ensete*, better known as the "Abyssinian Banana", and the *M. paradisiaca* (Fruiting Banana), both of which attain a height of between six and eight feet, were much favoured by the Victorians for growing in their renowned hot-houses. Today, they still make a striking and very elegant focal point in any spacious room, greenhouse or conservatory. Ample space is of paramount importance — the fairly broad and tall-growing leaves reach about three feet in length and twelve inches in width.

Despite its size and spread, the foliage is far from tough, indeed it is surprisingly brittle, which is one good reason why it is best to "mist" the delicate leaves clean, using a very fine aerosol spray. Never attempt to clean the leaves either quickly by hand, or with a leaf-shining agent, or they will tear! Lightly syringe them with water every day, which also helps to maintain a moist atmosphere, thus preventing both the leaves from browning at the tips and discouraging those white and woolly-looking mealy bugs which adhere to the axils and undersides of the older leaves. However, spraying alone is not always sufficient to ensure adequate humidity, so I take the additional precaution of standing the potted plants on a saucer, or a gravel base to which some water has been added. The water, which will be absorbed into the atmosphere, must be kept topped up, but the base of the pot must never be allowed to come in contact with the water-line, for "souring" of the compost or, worse still, root and stem rot will surely result.

Established plants can be purchased from nurseries which specialise in the more exotic varieties, but if you wish to rear your own specimens, you can obtain seed from many well-established horticultural firms. Germination can be speeded along by soaking the seeds in water for seventy-two hours, before sowing thinly in a tray containing seed compost. Cover them with a fine layer of compost, water thoroughly, and given a temperature of between 70° and 80°F (21°–27°C), they should sprout within a matter of three to four weeks.

Another means of propagating these charming plants is to detach the offsets which appear at the base of mature

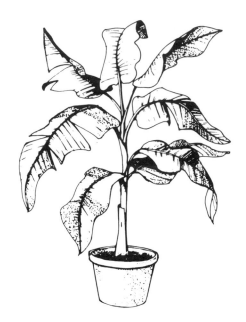

**Banana**

specimens. Once divided up these "babies" may be planted individually, in small porous flower plots containing J.I.P. No. 2 compost, and potted "on" into slightly larger containers when the roots become pot-bound. Plants which have passed the small stage, and are eighteen inches or more high, need a richer blend such as J.I.P. No. 3 compost. Given near ideal conditions, healthy specimens grow at a rate of over two feet per annum, and those growing in tubs and large containers need a more fertile mixture composed of equal parts of well-rotted humus and J.I.P. No. 3.

Unfortunately, decomposed matter contains harmful mites, and so it is important to sterilise it before using it (see page 17).

Banana plants do best in a very bright but sunless room, with a minimum winter temperature of around 60°F (15°C). Frequent watering is necessary during the height of the summer months, but whatever the season the compost must be allowed to become dry to the touch before re-watering. If this rule is not adhered to, all but aquatic plants will ultimately rot and die. Feed with a diluted liquid fertilizer every ten to fourteen days, from April to the beginning of September. Like people, plants generally benefit from a change in diet, so try to keep two or even three different brands of liquid fertilizer. By alternating them, you will be giving them the variety they so enjoy!

# Calathea

The botanical name *Calathea* has an interesting derivation, and is pertinent to these remarkably handsome plants. The name comes from the Greek work *kalathos* meaning a basket, and the leaves of some specimens are used by the natives of tropical America for weaving baskets. This seems a dreadful shame, and I would prefer it if these beautifully marked varieties were seen more frequently. The Peacock Plant (*C. makoyana*) is one of the better known varieties, both in England and America, and is almost instantly recognisable by the eyes (like those in the tail of a peacock) which are prominently displayed on the leaves.

Once you find that you can cope successfully with one specimen, you will, I am sure, look round for more beauties, like the Silver Calathea (*C. argyraea*), which has silvery-grey foliage with bright green veins. The Zebra Plant (*C. zebrina*) has green leaves with much darker green stripes, while the *C. louisae*, named after Queen Louise of the Belgians, has rich green foliage with a feathery design running along the central vein. This is often considered an easier specimen to manage, and is therefore more often seen in florists' and houseplant centres. Easier, yes, but none of the Calatheas could ever be thought of as an easy plant to look after, although a sunless position in a heated greenhouse or conservatory of at least 65°F (18°C), preferably 70°F (21°C), will go a long way towards easing the problem! Frequent sprayings of the foliage, a humid atmosphere (see pages 14–15), and a well-drained yet comfortably damp compost are also essential if you are to succeed and prevent the foliage becoming brown at the edges.

**Calathea**

When it comes to re-potting in March or April, a light and sterilised mixture (see page 17), of three parts of loam or J.I.P. No. 3, three parts of well-rotted leafmould, two parts of peat and two parts of sand is a rich and quick-draining compost.

# Chamaedorea elegans

*Dwarf Palm, Feather Palm, Parlour Palm*

Many palms are suitable for indoor culture, and yet they

eventually grow to such heights that it becomes impractical to keep them in most homes. The Dwarf Palm, however, as the popular name suggests, is one of the smallest, and the combination of the dwarf's convenient size and the lovely feather-like leaves has made it one of the better known varieties.

It is frequently sold under the name *neanthe bella*, but its correct botanical name is *Chamaedorea*, meaning "gift on the ground", because of the ease with which the natives of Mexico and Central America can harvest the bright scarlet fruits, which they eat, together with the young shoots of the plants. I am always loath to say that any plant will never produce flowers or fruit while growing indoors, but I have never heard of any privately-owned *Chamaedorea* doing so. Perhaps someone will be able to prove otherwise!

**Chamaedorea elegans**

Being a natural shade-lover, it lives in the wild under the protective branches of larger trees, where it can enjoy the close and moist atmosphere. Knowing how it lives in its native land helps us to understand how best to care for it. This love of humidity makes them ideal subjects for a terrarium or bottle garden, and being fairly slow to develop, they will not outgrow their home too quickly. Potted specimens enjoy frequent overhead showerings of tepid water, and this will help to keep the surrounding air moist and the foliage clean and free from aphids. When performing this task, it is best to hold the plant sideways so that you can spray the undersides of the leaves without soaking the compost. I have a lovely specimen which I water only when the top-soil becomes dry, for a constantly wet compost may result in a browning of the leaf tips, or even root rot which is far worse!

# Cissus antarctica

## *Kangaroo Vine*

This is a charming evergreen climber which is hardy and very rewarding to keep; it has masses of rich green and serrated leaves which taper to a point. Its Australian origin explains why it was christened Kangaroo Vine and it really does grow in leaps and bounds. I had one which grew to a height of nearly eight feet, and when I had trained its tendrils to a trellis support, it made a gorgeous room-divider.

However, those who wish to restrict it to a more workable size should keep it nearly pot-bound, and prune it back drastically each spring. A light yearly trimming is necessary, anyway, to remove unwanted shoots, and this can be combined with the propagating of healthy top-cuttings. Three-inch pieces should root easily in peat or sand, especially with a little bottom heat for encouragement, but to produce a really fine bushy second plant, pot several rooted cuttings together.

## Cissus antarctica

This vine grows best when kept in a coolish room of between 50° and 65°F (10° and 18°C). An over-hot and dry atmosphere can cause the foliage to turn brown at the edges, but a daily syringing of the leaves with tepid water will help to prevent this.

You will also need plenty of lukewarm water to quench this climber's thirst during the summer, although it is always best to allow the compost to become dry before re-watering. During the late autumn and winter, when the plant is resting, its demands are very different, and the compost should be kept on the dry side.

Spring is the best time to provide fresh J.I.P. No. 1 compost, but if you prefer to mix your own, a good home-blend consists of two parts of leafmould, one part of well-rotted manure, one part of loam, and half a part of coarse sand. For sterilising composts, (see page 17).

# Cordyline terminalis

*Tree of Kings, Flaming Dragon Tree, Ti Plant*

Growing in the wilds of South-East Asia, Australia and the Pacific Islands, this magnificent palm-like plant attains tree-like proportions, yet it rarely exceeds eighteen inches when kept in a pot. This is just as well, for if they proved to be rampant growers we would not see them frequently, if at all! Their beautiful pinky-red and green foliage is greatly sought after by flower arrangers.

**Cordyline terminalis**

Like many topical plants, the Tree of Kings needs humidity to flourish (see pages 14–15), and a daily syringing of the leaves, including the undersides, will keep it in fine fettle, and help to discourage Red Spider mites which might be around on any warm dry summer day. Immediately there are any signs of trouble, spray the leaves thoroughly with a suitable insecticide, such as liquid Derris or Malathion, and try to surround your specimen with a higher level of humidity. A sunless position in a temperature of around 60°F (15.5°C) is best, and in the summer months try to maintain a damp but not soggy compost. In autumn, when the plant will be preparing for its winter rest, watering should be drastically reduced until the spring — and, by the way, I always feed my own with pure rainwater. The *Cordyline* needs a rich and heavy growing mixture which drains quickly, and a well-crocked pot containing a sterilised mixture of three parts of J.I.P. No. 3, three parts of well-rotted leafmould, two parts of peat, and two parts of sand, will provide the club-shaped roots with ample nutriment.

Rooting two-inch pieces of main stem in the early part of the year will be difficult without some bottom heat of 70°–75°F (21°–24°C) for encouragement.

# Cryptanthus bivattus

*Earth Star Bromeliad*

Some months ago I was given a bag full of dying and dead plants which had been discarded by a well-known gardening centre, and amongst the mass of discoloured foliage and broken and tangled roots I came across two very sick-looking "Earth Star" bromeliads. Now, whilst on display, they had been knocked and broken off at the roots so that all that remained were two "topped" rosette-shaped "heads". I was in two minds whether to throw them out as being beyond even my imaginative ministrations when I had a brainwave! Standing them on top of a partially filled tumbler of water, I left them on the window-sill of my north-westerly facing bathroom, only disturbing them to top-up or change the fast evaporating water. Now remember these bromeliads had no roots at all. Yet, within a matter of weeks they had changed from a sick- and muddy-looking all-green colour to a gorgeous two-toned green with rose-pink overtones.

And that was not my only source of pleasure, for within that period each had also produced several small offsets from between its wavy leaves. In due course, when they were large enough to handle, several were removed and potted up, whilst the remaining ones were planted in one of my glass terrariums.

In the bathroom, of course, the surroundings are warm and naturally steamy. The damp air rose constantly from the plants' "seat" of moisture (the water) and enveloped them, and the bright yet sunless position helped the plants "back to life".

**Cryptanthus bivattus**

Most epiphytic bromeliads such as these have only a relatively small root growth, and living in the "jungle" conditions of the terrarium where the enclosed atmosphere is also moist and warm, and the compost damp, they are really thriving. Other jungle-like conditions can of course be fairly easily simulated in the home. After setting them in a quick-draining compost, and a semi-shaded position, you should spray the rosettes (not compost) once or twice a day with tepid water, and then they will flourish just like mine!

## Cyperus alternifolius

*Umbrella Plant, Umbrella Grass, Wood Rush*

Why this plant is so often seen in florists' when there are many more obviously attractive houseplants around at first seems a mystery. Yet when you look at it closely, and see its masses of leafed and umbrella-like stalks looking so uncultured, and so natural, you begin to understand its appeal, and can imagine it growing with the same abandon in the boggy wilds of Madagascar.

I think it always looks particularly beautiful when displayed around an indoor pool, or fountain, and it flourishes in the humid atmosphere. In fact, the Umbrella is one of the few plants which enjoys standing in water, although it is as well to remove excess liquid in the evening, and give it a fresh supply in a saucer or dish the following morning. The plant was introduced into Britain around 1780, and its height varies from one to six feet. It needs plenty of warmth, and although it can be kept in an ordinary living-room, the temperature should never drop below 55°F (13°C). A daily spraying of the foliage will prevent the leaves turning brown at the tips.

A specimen can be kept to a convenient height by pruning back each spring, and top sections which have a rosette of leaves and an inch of stem attached can be rooted easily in a moist and sandy compost. They may also be

**Cyperus alternifolius**

propagated by division of the roots, and when re-potting, use a fresh J.I.P. compost, preferably number 2, mixed with coarse sand, or alternatively, a blend of sterilised garden loam and coarse sand (see page 17).

Other strains you may come across are the *Cyperus diffusus*, which is often considered stronger and more compact, and its variegated counterpart *C.a. variegatus* which has cream and green striped leaves. A miniature form only grows to a height of about twelve inches (*C.a. gracilis*), and is ideal for decorating a very small pool. All of these require virtually the same treatment.

# Episcia

I cannot understand why these charming tropical American plants are not seen more often. Not only are they very attractive, with varied leaf markings, but they are reasonably easy to care for, and can be propagated either by division, or by rooting and detaching the smaller plants which form at the ends of thin shoots, like the Spider Plant (see page 41).

The low-growing Episcias make a lovely floor covering especially in a bottle garden or terrarium, which can provide a high level of humidity. A moist atmosphere is essential in an ordinary room, where the air is frequently very dry. A daily syringing over the foliage helps a lot, but to see how adequately to supply the right atmosphere turn to pages 14–15).

**Episcia**

I once saw a vivid display of these trailing plants hanging above a small indoor pool, and with their assorted pretty blooms they looked a picture. Their flowers are a real bonus, varying in shape, and ranging from an all-white, to a white-and-mauve speckled head, and on to the more brilliant scarlet and orange-red strains. For me, however, their variegated foliage is undoubtedly my first joy, and there are many gorgeous colour combinations. One of the better known Episcias is the *E. cupreata* with light green leaves which are relieved by a central vein of white, whilst the Chocolate Soldier is brown with white markings. The colouring of *E.c. metallica* reminds me of burnished copper, while E.c. Silver Sheen has a central silvery line on a rich background of bronze green.

There are many more strains, and all of them are happy in a room of about 65°F (18°C). Throughout the growing season give them adequate water with frequent doses of weak liquid fertiliser, but this must be discontinued during the winter, when the compost should be kept somewhat dry.

# Fatshedera lizei

*Fat-headed Lizzie, Ivy Tree, Climbing Fig-leaf Palm*

Those who find ivies appealing will undoubtedly love this charming evergreen, which is the result of a cross between the Irish Ivy (*Hedera helix hibernica*) and the Aralia (*Fatsia japonica*). A strong climber with leaves like the Aralia, but smaller, the *Fatshedera* is a real toughie, and will grow quite happily in most homes. A good environment for the *Fatshedera* is a coolish room of 55°F (13°c) or so, with regular liquid feeding throughout the growing months.

Some years ago I visited an acquaintance who loves two things in life — plants and paintings. I remember seeing a wall covered with nothing but watercolours, except for a rampant *Fatshedera*, which was clinging to and framing some of the pictures with its rich green foliage. It was a beauty which had been regularly pruned and refreshed with new J.I.P. No. 3 compost every spring. Any trimmed shoots had been rooted in water and then planted into the same pot which housed this thick and bushy specimen.

Whilst making plenty of foliage, it will need to be kept just moist with luke-warm water (never take the water

**Fatshedera lizei**

directly from the cold tap). The stems can grow to a height of six feet, and will need some support on which to cling—a trellis effect made from canes and raffia should be sufficient. The Ivy Tree, which was first seen in 1912, is hardy, but it still has its likes and dislikes. For instance, it enjoys being kept dust free by means of a soft wet sponge, yet hates to be cleaned with oily leaf-cleaning agents which can easily damage the foliage.

Although flowers are not a common occurrence, a mature specimen may bear clusters of small yellow-green heads, once it is several years old, so you might be lucky!

# Fatsia japonica

*Aralia, Fig-leaf Palm, False Castor Oil Plant*

I have had my Aralia for some years now. Although it has travelled around, finding itself in several different homes,

**109**

not once has it given us any worries. Any novices who are trying to select suitable indoor varieties for the first time should certainly try this wonderfully tolerant Japanese plant, which has attractive rich-green palmate leaves.

**Fatsia japonica**

As long as you avoid draughts — which will kill the hardest greenery — and always wait for the compost to dry out before watering again, the Aralia will put up with the slight failings of inexperience, and will probably look splendid into the bargain. Very large specimens will even grow out-of-doors in some mild areas, especially if planted in a shaded and protected spot. Even the smaller specimens will benefit from being placed outside during the summer months, but they should be positioned away from the sun, and brought inside well before the frosts come.

A cool room with a minimum winter temperature of 45°F (7°C) will keep the Aralia happy, for too hot an atmosphere can cause the foliage to turn yellow and fall. Each April, old compost may be replaced with a fresh blend of J.I.P. No. 3 and a little peat, and nipping out new

110

shoots, on a lanky specimen, will encourage it to sprout in the right places and become bushier.

Known to many as the False Castor Oil Plant, it should not be confused with the true oil-producing Castor Oil Plant (*Ricinus*) with larger bronze-green leaves. There is a very striking two-toned variety which has lighter-green delicately edged with cream. Unfortunately, it is only rarely seen, because, like many variegated plants, it is a slow grower and more delicate than its all-green counterpart.

## Ficus nekbudu

This particular Ficus, as any knowledgeable houseplant enthusiast will confirm, is certainly not an easy subject to grow successfully — probably due to the fact that very little has been written concerning its culture.

One of the main causes for general concern is the way the foliage turns yellow, and falls without warning during the winter months. I have had my own two-and-a-half feet tall specimen for over three years, yet fortunately have not suffered any such problem. Indeed, the one and only time I lost a leaf occurred when I was attempting to clean the foliage. Unlike the more common strains of Ficus, the leaves of this variety are far more brittle than they appear, and although I was particularly gentle when sponging them clean, one young leaf suddenly snapped in half. Since then I have taken no chances, and use only a very light overhead misting device to clean the dark green top growth.

An unexpected leaf-loss can easily be caused by sudden variations in watering, and room temperature. Aim to keep the compost fairly dry during the winter, and only increase the volume of water gradually during the warmer months.

111

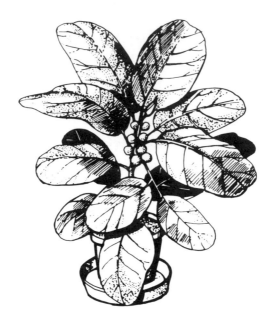

## Ficus nekbudu

Throughout the year my Ficus grows well in a very cool room of around 60°F (15.5°C), and this is possibly the reason why it has never been invaded by scale insects. They love the strain, and can prove a very real problem if given the chance. The majority of pests do not like cool and humid conditions, but any attack, however mild, should be treated quickly with liquid Derris or Malathion — mild soapy water will also sometimes do the trick — before they get a stranglehold.

When re-potting in the spring, try not to succumb to the natural inclination to "over-pot" and simply provide your plant with a porous container which is just large enough snugly to encompass the root system and growing mixture. Old compost should be renewed annually, using either J.I.P. Nos. 2 and 3, or a mixture of two parts of J.I.P. No. 2, one part of sterilised and well-rotted leafmould (see page 17), one part of peat, and one part of coarse sand. To this you can add a small pinch of bone-meal.

# Fittonia

Although they are not extremely easy, the Fittonias should not prove impossible, particularly if you use a little cunning. They can be successfully reared enclosed in a terrarium, a clear glass pickling jar, or even a goldfish bowl (without the fish of course!) and then the going is simple.

To understand the Fittonias, you must imagine them growing in the monsoon climate of Peru, where a moist warm atmosphere prevails. Then, by providing a similar humidity in your home (see page 17), with a minimum temperature of 65°F (18°C), you will more than win the battle! A barely moist compost is fine, for too much water, especially during the dormancy period, will quickly rot and kill any specimen.

**Fittonia**

They grow better when regularly re-potted each spring; I have tried several recipes, two of which seem to work very well. The first is a blend of equal parts of J.I.P. No. 2 and peat, and the other is a mixture of two parts of J.I.P.

No. 1 and one part of rich loam. (For sterlising compost see page 17). They have a small root-ball so when re-housing use a well-crocked pot which will give adequate drainage, while holding the roots just snugly, and so avoid both over-potting and squashing them.

The Fittonias take their name from the two sisters. Elisabeth and Sarah Mary Fitton, joint authors of the once popular *Conversations of Botany* in 1817. There are two varieties worth mentioning. The *Fittonia verschaffeltii Argyroneura*, or, as it is more frequently called, the Nerve Plant, is an easily obtainable trailing variely. The nickname stems from the fact that the light-green foliage is delicately broken up by a mass of fine silver veins. I can never decide which of the two I prefer because the equally prominent markings of the *Fittonia verschaffeltii* (Mosaic Plant) — deep red veining on a darker green background — make this one a very striking-looking specimen, too.

# Maranta leuconeura kerchoveana

*Prayer Plant, Ten Commandment Plant, Rabbit's Tracks*

This is one of the better known varieties of Maranta, and it has several popular names, all of which are perfectly ascribed to this very attractive and compact plant. It is known in England as the Prayer Plant because of its habit of folding its leaves like hands in prayer, whilst in America the name Ten Commandments refers to the ten chocolate-coloured blotches which run in pairs on either side of the central vein.

Discovered in tropical America, the Maranta is a very easy plant to nurture if it is placed in a humid atmosphere of between 60° and 65°F (15.5° and 18°C), away from

## Maranta leuconeura kerchoveana

draughts and direct sunshine. This is not always possible in the home, but if they are planted in a terrarium they will flourish with very little attention. Many do grow happily as single specimens, especially if the foliage and roots are kept well sprayed and moist throughout the summer months. Spraying the leaves is beneficial all the year round, but in winter the roots should be kept almost dry.

Always try to provide your plant with fresh compost each spring, using either J.I.P. No. 2, or a sterilised mixture of equal parts of leafmould, peat and sand. (For sterilising compost see page 17). Only re-pot your plant when the roots are pot-bound, and then a one-size larger pot will be sufficient. If it is deep, a good portion of it should be filled with crocks before adding your compost. You can propagate from any large specimen at the same time, by dividing the underground stems (rhizomes) into sections, which should be planted separately.

Another real beauty which requires the same care is the *Maranta leuconeura erythrophylla*, or Fish-Bone Plant, which came from Brazil in 1875. The rich green foliage

**115**

has striking red veins, the central one being edged with a lighter green.

# Monstera deliciosa

## *Swiss Cheese Plant*

It is not often that large foliage plants rank high in the popularity stakes, but the Monstera is an exception. Its main appeal lies in the beauty of the large green serrated leaves and the thick aerial roots, and it is not difficult to imagine it growing in the jungles of tropical America.

Naturally, the fact that it is such a tolerant plant also has its attractions, but providing it with good growing conditions will greatly enhance it, and may encourage it to produce exotic-looking fruit. These, which slightly resemble a skinned banana with a comb-like finish, are edible, and the pulp tastes rather like a pineapple. It is not an every-day occurrence to see these plants flowering and fruiting in the home, but it is certainly not impossible either. One of the finest privately owned specimens I have ever seen was a gargantuan example growing in a conservatory, and producing several fruits at the same time.

The aerial roots, which grow from the stem, are best directed into the compost as soon as they are long enough. There they should root and provide an added source of nutriment, but until they are of sufficient length you can keep the plant looking tidy by tying them to the main stem.

The Swiss Cheese enjoys a temperature of around 65°F (18°C), and, during the growing period, regular doses of liquid fertiliser. Young folded leaves should not be touched because it is easy to damage them, but mature leaves should be kept dust-free, preferably with a soft sponge dipped in tepid water. Luke-warm water should also be used when watering the compost, and allowing the top-soil to become dry in between waterings will help to prevent both root rot and discolouration of the foliage, both of which are caused by excess moisture.

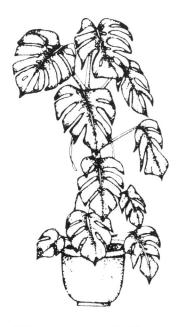

**Monstera deliciosa**

# Nephrolepsis exaltata

The *Nephrolepsis exaltata* (Ladder Fern), and the many cultivars produced by cross-breeding, are amongst the largest and loveliest of all the popular indoor ferns. The name "exaltata" means "tall and lofty looking", obviously a reference to the decorative pinnate fronds which reach an average height of two feet.

The Nephrolepsis ferns vary enormously in both leaf

117

shape and tone, the *Nephrolepsis exaltata* having pale-green fronds, whilst an earlier mutant, the fast-growing *N.e. Bostoniensis* (Boston Fern) had broader feathery-like foliage. Another elegant beauty, the *N.e. Elegantissima*, has tripinnate to quadripinnate fronds of bright green, which give it a rather lovely fluffy effect. The curled and crinkled light-to-mid-green fronds of *N.e. Hillii* may reach three feet in length, and other readily available cultivars include the *N.e. Marshallii* (pale green), the *N.e. Whitmanii*, commonly known as the Lace Fern, the *N.e. Rooseveltii plumosa* which has wavy fronds, and the *N.e. Fluffy Ruffles*, a smaller-growing form, the fluffy fronds of which reach a mere twelve inches in length.

**Nephrolepsis exaltata**

Any of these species may be planted together in a hanging basket lined with sphagnum moss, and containing equal parts by volume of J.I.P. No. 2, leafmould, peat and sand. (To sterilise see page 17.) Alternatively, they may be set individually in four- or five-inch pots containing a compost consisting of three parts of J.I.P. No. 2, three parts of peat, and one part of sharp sand.

All of them grow well in a light yet sunless position, and when given a minimum temperature of 50°F (10°C), they are long-lived, even when temporarily neglected. When deprived of essential water the foliage will brown and die, but new growth will soon appear once all the dead fronds are removed and the compost watered regularly. From April to the end of September the compost must be watered freely, and a weak solution of liquid fertiliser fed to them once every two weeks. For the rest of the year, however, from September until the following spring, all fertiliser feeding must be withheld, and the liquid reduced sufficiently to keep the compost no more than damp. Regular overhead and light spraying will keep the greenery healthy and dust-free.

During the summer months the creeping stems send up "stolons" which produce more young plants. These may be propagated by separating them from the parent plants, and potting them into two inch pots containing a rooting mixture of equal parts of peat and sand. Given a "bottom" heat of 55°F (13°C), they will root readily, and will then be ready for planting on into a more suitable growing medium.

# Pellionia

Keep an eye out for these lovely little plants from South-East Asia, because not only are they easy to manage, but when hung on the wall they make a charming and effective trailing display. We call them Curiosity Plants because on our return from holiday one year we found that not only had they trailed over the sides of their own pot, but spread, and rooted in the two containers below. Maybe they wondered where we were, or more likely thought it a good opportunity to have a look round undisturbed.

They grow better when kept well away from the summer sun, in a room of at least 60°F (15.5°C), and a reasonably high humidity (see pages 14–15), and a daily overhead showering with tepid water will keep them content. Their compost, a light and porous blend of J.I.P. No. 1 and peat, must be kept pleasantly damp throughout the warmer months, but in the autumn it should be much drier.

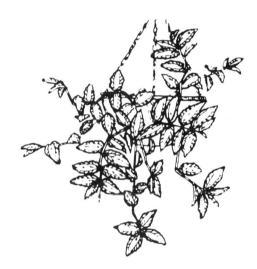

### Pellionia

Almost any time throughout the summer, two-inch cuttings will root very easily in a moist and sandy mixture, or longer stems may be pegged down into their own pots, as mine did naturally. Once they have put down their anchors, they can be severed from the established plant and re-potted into the J.I.P. growing medium.

The two cousins which you are most likely to come across are the *Pellionia daveauana* and the *Pellionia pulchra.* The *P. daveauana* was named after the nineteenth-century director of the Lisbon Botanical Gardens, Jules Daveauana, and has almost oval leaves between one and two inches long. These are delicately shaded with a green centre which graduates towards a bronzy-green nearer the edges, whilst the *P. pulchra* is more heavily veined, with a silvery-green finish. Of the two this latter one is often considered to be the more suitable for the home.

# Peperomia

The size of this Pepper family made it almost impossible to pick just one plant to include in this book, as they are all so varied and appealing.

Found in the jungles of Central and tropical America, they grow at the base of trees, and although they do not need intense heat, they like a minimum of 55°F or 60°F (13° or 15.5°C). They have fairly thick leaves, and so can go for some time without water, and then only small amounts are needed to sustain the small root growth. To

**Peperomia**

prevent rotting, always allow the compost to become dry, and then wait a couple of days before re-watering.

In the wild they enjoy high humidity, and this must be provided and maintained in the home (see pages 14–15). This problem is easily overcome if you plant them in a terrarium. I once filled a large discarded fish tank with nothing but these jungle plants, and the effect was stunning. Some were supported on pieces of cork bark halfway up the sides, whilst others were planted at graduated levels to give variety of height.

Each spring, potted specimens will benefit from a fresh mixture of J.I.P. No. 3 and a little peat, and with some bottom heat, many may be propagated without much trouble. Detach a leaf with some stalk, or a stem cutting, and plant them in a moist and sandy mixture.

Varieties which are easily available include the Emerald Green (*P. caperata*) and the Desert Privet (*P. magnifolia*), the Ivy (*P. hederifolia*), and the trailing cream *Peperomia glabella variegata*. The Emerald Green has a rich green and crinkled foliage, unlike the smoother, cream and green leaves of the Desert Privet, while the Ivy has beautiful greyish-green leaves with a shiny metallic finish. With so many other varieties also available, there is something to suit everyone.

# Philodendron bipinnatifidum

*Tree Philodendron*

The Tree Philodendron is not a climber, but it needs a fairly wide area in which to spread its rich-green and shiny palm-shaped leaves. In California these are often seen outside on patios and terraces, but in a more inclement climate they need a steady indoor temperature of at least

122

65°F (18°C), coupled with the same humidity in which they thrive in the dank rain forests of Brazil (see pages 14–15). I hope one day to have another large conservatory, devoted to this strikingly handsome tropical family.

Their compost, a quick-draining and light mixture of two parts of J.I.P. No. 1, one and a half parts of leafmould, one part of coarse sand, and half a part of peat, must be sterilised before use (see page 17). During the hotter months especially, the roots should be thoroughly watered, and then allowed to become almost dry before the treatment is repeated, but as the colder months approach less frequent and smaller quantities will be called for. Like all its relatives, the Tree Philodendron hates a constantly soggy growing medium, and will do far better in a well-crocked pot with a plentiful supply of drainage holes.

**Philodendron bipinnatifidum**

Any aerial roots which appear should be directed back into the compost, as soon as they are long enough, for they will provide the plant with a useful conveyor belt for food. This does not mean that regular feeding with a branded fertiliser is unnecessary. On the contrary, it should prove extremely beneficial, but remember, only feed it when the plant is producing its beautiful leaves.

# Philodendron leichtinii

This particular Philodendron is not new to indoor culture, and yet there seems to have been comparatively little written about it. No doubt it is due to the general lack of information that these very lovely plants really seem to suffer, for all too often they can be seen under the weather, their once rich and deep green leaves horribly discoloured, dry and brittle. Because of all this, I feel some sort of a "yardstick" for their care is very much overdue, and I only hope that relating my own experience with them will help at least some other owners, well before the foliage gets to such a sad and sorry state.

The oval leaves have numerous neatly cut holes in them — almost as though some tidy-minded marching marauder has been systematically munching its way over the whole plant — and are somewhat similar to the mature foliage of some Swiss Cheese Plants (*Monsteras*). Actually this species is almost known genetically as a "Monstera", and it is generally believed that both species actually originated in similar climatic regions, the holed foliage enabling the plants to withstand the extremely windy conditions without causing them any serious damage.

My specimens seem happiest in a comfortably heated room of around 70°F (21°C), but I was very relieved when they did not die or even appear to suffer much when, during the very coldest part of the winter, we were without any central heating fuel for three days, and the temperature must have dropped by 20°F! I treat them in exactly the

## Philodendron leichtinii

same way as all my Philodendrons by regular overhead misting and watering the compost whenever it looks almost dry. This sort of care, with a moist atmosphere, and lightly-shaded rooms, should keep them at their perky peak!

Slow growers they are supposed to be, but if your experience is the same as mine you certainly would not believe it! Last summer, one of mine almost took over a corner of the lounge. Do not hesitate to prune them as soon as they show signs of getting "leggy", they will quickly sprout new growth!

# Philodendron scandens

*Sweetheart Vine, Bathroom Plant*

In Great Britain, this climber is best known for its romantic heart-shaped leaves, perhaps because under the cool exterior lies a warm romantic streak! Throughout America, however, it is referred to as the Bathroom Plant, and this is understandable for that room, especially if frequently used, provides a near-perfect environment. With regular bathing and showering producing plenty of moist air, and a temperature which rarely drops below 65°F (18°C), this favourite is in its element!

**Philodendron scandens**

The Sweetheart can, of course, live successfully in any sunless part of the house, as long as the atmosphere is sufficiently humid (see page 17), and a daily all-over spraying with luke-warm water will help a lot. Although originally discovered in Central America, it is also a native of the West Indies, and being a vigorous climber (it can reach a height of over six feet) it requires some artificial means of support. A rolled-up piece of wire netting filled with live and wet sphagnum moss, a moss-covered pole, or any strong structure with a moisture-holding material on which the aerial roots may cling and feed will be good.

A compost of peat and sand will suffice, but to rear a giant calls for a richer and equally porous compost of two parts of J.I.P. No. 1, one and a half parts of leafmould, one part of coarse sand, and half a part of peat. (For sterilising see page 17.) Try to keep the compost comfortably damp, and fed with liquid fertiliser in the summer, and remember that these tropical plants live in the protected shade of dense forests, so they will not appreciate any direct exposure to the sun! It is, however, extremely tolerant of gas and oil fumes.

# Phoenix dactylifera

This is a well-known palm, the boughs of which appear rather stiff and more spiky than the majority of its kind, and it is better known as the Date Palm. The stones of any whole dates left over from Christmas should be washed and popped into the deep freeze for a week or so — surprisingly enough this cold treatment encourages germination — before setting them in a sandy compost, in a temperature of 64°–70°F (18°–21°C). After about eight or ten weeks you should see the tiny heads pushing through the compost, and once the seedlings are large enough to handle, they should be re-potted singly into three-inch pots, containing a blend of three parts of J.I.P. No. 1, and one part of fine sand.

Palms grow best when the roots are confined to a limited area, and so it is only necessary to transfer them into one-size larger pots each time their roots become pot-bound — probably once a year during the growing season. They are often slow to "get going", but by nature they are fairly fast growers when they have started, and the young seedlings will take only three or four years to become medium-sixed specimens. If you cannot wait, however, large and well-established plants are available from florists' shops and nurseries.

**Phoenix dactylifera**

In winter they require good light and a minimum temperature of 55°F (13°C). Water should be given only sparingly, keeping the compost barely damp until April when the quantity of water must be slowly increased. Feeding every two or three weeks with a houseplant fertiliser may also be resumed, and continued through the summer. As the months pass, and the sun increases in intensity, a light but sunless position is called for. Quite frequently, I pop mine outside in a shaded part of the garden where they benefit from the natural light, fresh air, and a regular overhead spraying which helps to keep the foliage fresh, clean and pest-free.

# Platycerium bifurcatum

*Stag Horn Fern, Elk-Horn*

It is often believed that divided front-leaves are a character-istic common to all ferns. This is not correct, for there are many species which look like foliage plants, and the Stag Horn Fern is one.

This Australian fern was originally discovered in 1808 and is a fascinating and easy plant to keep, possessing two types of leaves, both of which have an essential role to play in the plant's survival. The rounded, flattish ones serve as an anchor, by wrapping themselves around a tree branch or other support. These are sterile, and it is the more decorative antler-shaped fronds which produce the spores. The botanical name *Platycerium* comes from the two Greek words meaning "wide horn", and refers to the lovely trailing "antlers" which have a rich green and downy finish.

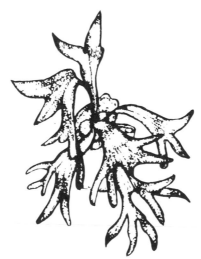

**Platycerium bifurcatum**

These ferns look impressive when displayed in hanging

baskets, and several specimens planted together can be suspended from a greenhouse or conservatory ceiling. Alternatively, they can be removed from their pots, their root-ball encased between two pieces of cork bark, and hung on a wall in a shaded position.

To water them sufficiently you should submerge them in a bowl of tepid water, preferably rain-water, until the small root-system is thoroughly soaked, but always allow the compost to become nearly dry between waterings. Daily light sprayings will provide some humidity (see pages 14-15), and will also keep the foliage clean without harming the soft downy texture — as some leaf cleaning agents might do. They will need a damp atmosphere, and a fairly warm one as well. A minimum 65°F (18°C) is all right, although a few degrees higher will be better. In the late spring, they can be safely replanted into a pot containing ample crocks with a mixture of equal parts of sphagnum moss and peat. Give them regular weak doses of liquid fertiliser.

# Rhoicissus rhomboidea

*Grape Ivy, Natal Vine*

This member of the Vine family is very versatile; you can train it to climb up a trellis, or leave it to trail down without support, or maintain it as a bushy specimen by pruning any top growth as soon as it appears. Any beheaded healthy pieces which have a couple of leaves and a short stalk can be rooted fairly easily in the spring, and if four or five cuttings are potted together, they will soon make a fine plant.

The Grape Ivy's popularity is due to the richness of the leaves, each of which is composed of three serrated leaflets,

**Rhoicissus rhomboidea**

and to its hardiness. I never realised how resilient this plant is until I saw one in the home of an elderly lady. She had no other plants, and how this very weedy scraggy-looking object survived was a mystery! It was so dark, cold and draughty in her hallway that I would not have believed any plant could have stayed the course! Do not think from this story, however, that you can now push them into a dingy corner in the belief that they will flourish, come what may.

Good conditions will always produce better specimens, and this one is happiest during the hotter months in a room temperature of around 60°F (15.5°C), although in the winter it may safely drop 10°F (5°C) or so. While it is growing the compost should be kept moist, and occasionally fed with fertiliser.

Try to ensure that a humid atmosphere is maintained at all times (see pages 14–15), and if your Grape Ivy is

131

happy it may produce little grape-like berries — do not worry, they are not poisonous. Gas fumes cause the deaths of many plants, but this one will not suffer any ill-effects from such appliances.

# Saxifraga sarmentosa

*Mother-of-Thousands, Strawberry Geranium*

If you love propagating plants you will need plenty of space to keep up with the Mother-of-Thousands, which, as its name suggests, produces hundreds of babies in a lifetime! These plantlets form on long, fine threads, and look very appealing when trailing over the sides of a wall container where they can hang freely. Some months ago, I put one of my indoor specimens outside in the garden, and several birds decided that these dangling leaves would make ideal nesting material, and flew off with the cords. Make sure you never make the same mistake!

**Saxifraga sarmentosa**

Although the hanging runners are extremely decorative

as they are, they can be pegged down into a second pot containing moist peat or coarse sand, and when they have rooted, the cord from the parent plant can be severed. Then you can re-pot them in a standard growing mixture, and put them in a coolish room of between 50° and 60°F (10° and 15.5°C). If you want to encourage the sprays of tiny white flowers which appear on twelve-inch stems during the summer, the plant will need lots of shaded light, and whilst it is making plenty of new foliage, the compost is best kept damp. Regular doses of liquid fertiliser will help. With little growth during the winter, however, less water will be required, and feeding should be completely stopped until the following spring.

It was because of its similarity to the Strawberry plant that it became known as the Strawberry Geranium, but its Latin name, *Saxifraga*, means "breaker of rocks", and could refer to its liking for rocky nooks and crannies in the wild. There is an intriguing belief that the hairy leaves when boiled make an effective potion for gall-stones!

# Sonerila margaritacea

A native of Java, this plant is an extremely difficult variety to cultivate successfully, because the majority of homes are subject to draughts, fluctuating temperatures, and over-dry atmospheres, and it only takes one or a combination of these unfavourable conditions to cause the plant to drop its leaves and possibly die.

The easiest way to overcome some of these difficulties, and provide the plant with perfect damp, warm and humid conditions, is to plant it in a terrarium with other low-growing varieties. With its lovely oval and silvery leaves, the undersides of which are purple, and the reddish stems, it will do very well, and also provide the vital colour contrast which is so often lacking in many mixed arrangements. A helpful alternative is first to place a small container of water alongside the potted specimen, and then cover both the plant and water-holder with a large upturned transparent jar. The result is an ideal enclosed moist and draught-free atmosphere, but the water level must be maintained at all times.

Using this latter method will greatly minimise the risk of failure, but it is necessary to ensure that your Sonerila is carefully and sensibly watered. Throughout the summer it requires quite a lot of water, but during the dormant winter period, only sufficient moisture to keep the plant healthy. Over-watering will quickly prove fatal, so to obtain the correct balance, simply follow the golden rule — re-water only when the compost feels quite dry, and not before! If the leaves suddenly shrivel for no apparent reason, it will be a sure sign that the light is far too bright, and the plant should be moved to a more shaded spot.

Each spring re-pot your specimen in a fresh, quick-

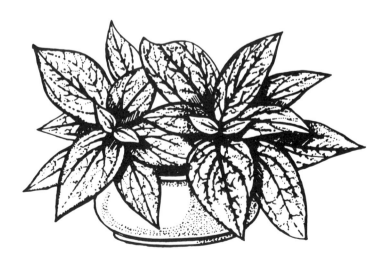

**Sonerila margaritacea**

draining growing medium, such as a peat-based compost. A good mixture, which I make up myself, consists of two parts of J.I.P. No. 2, one part of peat, and one part of coarse sand.

# Sparmannia africana

*African Wind Flower, African Hemp, Window Linden*

A member of the lime family, this vigorous climber was named after the botanist Andreas Sparman, who, in the 1770s, joined Captain Cook on his second voyage to New Zealand. The African Wind Flower grows wild in the marshes and bogs of South Africa, often reaching a height of more than twenty feet, and in the summer produces masses of white flowers with purple stamens. Although these are rather delicate, and only last for a day or so, they open up at the slightest sign of wind, to aid pollination — hence its name. It is happy in a slightly shaded or a brighter light, as long as it is protected from the summer sun, and it adapts reasonably well to ordinary living-room conditions. However, the ideal winter temperature of around 60°F (15.5°C) should never be allowed to drop more than 10°F (5°C).

I have sometimes been asked how a specimen can be made to bloom again. You should give it a rest in the summer, after blooming has finished. At this time, no liquid food should be given, and watering should be limited to a minimum. During this period all the foliage will fall but do not be alarmed because after a month or so the plant will sprout again, especially after a good pruning.

After re-potting it in a well-crocked pot containing J.I.P. No. 3, watering and feeding may be resumed gradually. Given this period of semi-hibernation, nearly all plants

**135**

**Sparmannia africana**

over a year old will flower annually. An over-hot and dry atmosphere may cause the gorgeous bright green leaves to turn yellow, so try to supply some all-the-year-round humidity (see pages 14–15). Old plants may be replaced with younger and bushier specimens, by rooting several cuttings, and potting them together at any time during the growing season.

# Stromanthe amabilis

Many of you will no doubt have noticed that this exquisite-looking plant, which has beautifully marked two-toned green leaves with mauve undersides, greatly resembles the Maranta and Calathea group of plants.

This similarity in appearance is hardly surprising for it is closely related, and consequently enjoys similar growing conditions. Like the two main strains of Marantas, it likes a well-shaded light position, and if given too bright a spot will quickly suffer a browning and curling of the leaves. This specimen enjoys a warm growing environment, and consequently it is always advisable to keep a close eye on the compost, particularly during the summer months when more water will be needed to sustain the developing plant. Always allow the compost to become almost but not quite dry between waterings, and this rule applies during both the summer and winter. A reasonably high and constant humidity is essential throughout the year, and by employing the well-known and conventional means of using either moistened sphagnum moss, wet peat, or a trayful of gravel to which some water has been added, this necessary state may be achieved with little trouble or expense. Always aim to keep the foliage fresh, clean, and pest-free with a daily overhead "misting" using a fine aerosol.

**Stromanthe amabilis**

The *Stromanthe amabilis* needs a very open and porous compost, otherwise the roots cannot breathe, and one which you can easily make yourself consists of four parts of J.I.P. No. 2, two parts of peat, and two parts of sand. Because of their creeping rhizomes, very large specimens are propagated by removing them from their pots and simply dividing the roots into a number of smaller sections. These in turn are potted up into small two-and-a-half or three-inch pots, containing a mixture of three parts of J.I.P. No. 1 and one part each of peat and sand. Keep the compost damp, and pot on into a one-size larger pot (a three-and-a-half-inch or five-inch pot as the case may be) only when the roots have become pot-bound and are starting to show through the drainage hole, not before!

# Syngonium

## *Goose Foot*

Both in England and the U.S.A. the lovely Syngoniums are sometimes incorrectly labelled and sold under the name of *Nephthytis*, yet few of us could ever mistake the very distinctive foliage which looks like the feet of a goose. They come from the wilds of Central and South America, and, like the Philodendrons, are essentially climbers or creepers, attaching themselves by tendrils to any porous mass which they encounter. This gives them not only a support but also a reservoir of moisture upon which to feed, and this is worth remembering when rearing them in a pot. They grow far better when given a moist sphagnum moss stick or a piece of cork bark, which must be dampened each day.

My mother has a magnificent specimen growing on a bark-covered tree branch, with other large plants protecting it from the sun's rays, in a temperature of 65°F (18°C). I doubt if her Goose Foot realises that it has even left its homeland! This plant is not difficult, as long as a constant minimum 60°F (15.5°C) — 65°F (18°C) is better — can be maintained. As with so many others, a reasonable humidity is essential (see pages 14–15), and the growing medium — I use a blend of J.I.P. No. 1 and peat-moss — should never be re-watered until it is quite dry.

**Syngonium**

Many mature specimens can reach heights of five feet or so, but they can also be restricted easily by lopping off the tops at the desired level. The resultant cuttings, with a leaf or two attached, can be dipped in a hormone rooting powder, and potted up, whereupon they will root without difficulty. It is always good to have new plants coming on, to take the place of the older ones once they are past their prime. Young and old alike will grow better if fed regularly with a branded fertiliser throughout the leaf-producing months.

# Tolmiea menziesii

*Pickaback Plant, Piggyback Plant*

The Piggyback could never be called exotic, and to

many people the soft green and hairy foliage would not even seem pretty, yet this little plant has a hidden charm. It appeal lies in the plantlets which grow in the centre of each leaf, and if these are allowed to remain, one will end up with a lovely trailing plant, all the leaves carrying several generations of babies on their backs! In the wild state the older leaves bearing the offspring eventually rest on the ground, and rot, leaving behind the young and already rooted plant. We can rear these plantlets by removing them and pegging them into an ordinary potting compost. Alternatively, any large specimen can be divided into several smaller portions, at any time during the late spring or summer months.

During the growing period these North American plants require ample watering. If they are allowed to become completely dry for only a short time they will wilt quickly. They do perk up just as speedily once their thirst has been quenched, but try not to leave them without moisture for too long. They are simple plants to look after and will

**Tolmiea menziesii**

grow happily in a room of between 50° and 55°F (10°C and 13°C), but keep them away from the sun.

If you care properly for the *Tolmiea*, you may be rewarded with tiny green and purple flowers. Although it is kept for the decorative appearance of the leaves, like many foliage plants it does produce blooms during the summer months.

# CHAPTER
# TWELVE

# Flowering plants — moderately easy

## Aechmea fasciata

*Urn Plant, Exotic Brush*

When I was a teenager I bought my grandmother a lovely large Urn Plant which, even then, was considered very pricey. I bought it because I liked it — a mistake we have all made at some time — and I did not consider that this Brazilian bromeliad might not take to Nan's home, which was always considered a little chilly for the rest of the family although Nan never felt cold, but I reckon that poor plant did because its spell in that house was very short lived!

I could not have chosen a less suitable variety, for it dislikes temperatures which fall below 60°F (15.5°C), and with Nan's constant streams of "good fresh air" in winter and summer, it must have suffered agonies! The Urn thrives with central heating, but needs its little water container in the middle of the rosette kept well filled with soft tepid water. Occasional weak quantities of liquid fertiliser may be added, but it is best always to leave the actual compost only moist, never wet, because in the wild these epiphytes live on trees, and do not really require soil

### Aechmea fasciata

in which to exist. Their food supply is the warm dew which fills their vase, and their roots are used mainly as an anchor.

Owners who wish either to re-pot their existing specimen, or to transplant the offshoots once they have reached a decent size, may use a mixture of equal parts of peat-moss, osmunda fibre, and decomposed leafmould, with sufficient sand to make it open textured and porous. The pot used does not need to be extremely large, but it must offer ample drainage by being well-crocked. The *Aechmea* was introduced into Britain in 1826. It wants a shaded yet light siting, with lots of fresh air, but no draughts!

# Allamanda

When I first became absorbed in the world of plants I read all the indoor plant books on which I could lay my hands, but only rarely did I come across any mention of the Allamandas. Certainly British books seem to neglect them,

but in Holland the variety called *Allamanda cathartica* —
the Golden Trumpet — is far better known and is seen
much more frequently indoors. This genus of shrubs is
found in South America and the West Indies, and the roots
of one of them — the pinkish-purple blooming *Allamanda
violacea* — are used in Brazil to allay fevers. The *A.
violacea* was introduced into England in 1850, and the
Golden Trumpet, from Guyana, has been in cultivation a
little longer, since 1785.

Both varieties are climbers, and in the tropics they are
trained into hedges, which provide a wonderful summer
and autumn screen of lilac and yellow trumpet-shaped
flowers. One likely reason for their unpopularity is that
the blooms are poisonous and must be kept out of the
reach of children.

Named after the Swiss botanist, Frederik Allamand,
these beauties are reasonably ease to maintain, but it is not
always simple to root them from cuttings, though with
several three-inch shoots potted in a sandy mixture and

tightly covered with polythene, you may stand a reasonable chance. Any "successes" you obtain can then be transferred to a more suitable houseplant compost. Warm and light rooms of at least 60°F (15.5°C) offer the most favourable conditions, but if the windows are facing directly south or west the plants will need some shading in the warmer months. Humidity (see pages 14–15) and enough water to maintain a damp growing mixture is the required treatment throughout the year.

# Begonia haageana

## *Elephant's Ear Begonia*

Begonias have always been a well-loved genus, and anyone who has already grown some of the unusual varieties might like to try his or her hand with the "Elephant's Ear". A taller grower than most, this magnificent plant may reach a height of up to six feet, and always makes a beautiful show with both its foliage and blossoms.

The leaves which have red undersides and are covered with fine red hairs are striking enough, but throughout the summer and autumn the clusters of shell-pink, pendulous blooms lend such loveliness that one wonders if Saint Catherine herself had a hand in their evolution. I suppose she did in an indirect way because it was on her island, the Santa Catherina Island in Brazil, where this plant was first discovered by a Herr Scharff. Yet the seeds themselves were first found in a mixed consignment sent to Kew by the horticultural firm of Haage and Schmidt of Erfurt, Germany who expressed the desire that any new varieties found should be named after Herr Scharff, their founder. Unfortunately, all their hopes were dashed forever when,

**Begonia haageana**

in 1888, the Gardeners Chronicle published an article on this Begonia which had already been christened *B. haageana*. Botanically, this could not be righted, and so it has been known ever since by this name, although it is still sometimes referred to as *B. scharfii*.

The "Elephant's Ear" is certainly no weakling where heat, or rather the lack of it, is concerned, for it will withstand winter temperatures as low as 45°F (7°C). Under such conditions, however, the compost is best on the dry side, but in higher temperatures, particularly when the specimen is producing foliage and flowers, the soil should be comfortably moist most of the time.

Once, I saw one of these Begonias standing in the window of a high-ceilinged living room, and it was a spectacular sight — facing west as it did — north is just as good — the plant received all the light it needed without roasting in the hot summer sun.

146

# Begonia metallica

## *Metal-leaf Begonia*

The Metal-leaf Begonia is a charming specimen, even without the shell-pink and white flowers which, although not as striking as those of some Begonias, are still an attractive part of the plant during the autumn. The leaves have a bronze-green metallic-like surface, and the plant may sometimes reach a height of three to four feet, but please do not allow it to become long and lanky like the one I saw recently. This individual had never been pruned, but it had the makings of something quite impressive, if the owner were to lop off the top six inches or so.

They are not particularly vigorous growers, but in the spring they can be generously pruned, to give a full and more luxuriant growth. At the same time, re-pot them either in J.I.P. No. 3, or you can blend two parts of loam, two parts of peat, two parts of leafmould, and one and a half parts of sand. (For sterilising such mixtures see page

**Begonia metallica**

17.) Cuttings, three to four inches long, will often root easily in peat and sand, but must be potted later into a more suitable growing mixture.

Even more than most Begonias, the Metal-leaf must have ample shade in the sunnier months, and it will flourish in a moderately-heated room, despite being a native of a very hot and sunny country, Brazil. In winter, the cooler their surroundings are, the less water they will take. Never leave them entirely without, but keep them fairly dry. In the summer you may be more free with their liquid intake, as long as you keep the water well away from the foliage.

# Beloperone guttata

## *Shrimp Plant*

This fascinating indoor shrub with decorative bracts is referred to throughout Europe as the Shrimp, because the tiny oval-shaped leaves, which overlap each other, very much resemble the little sea creature in both shape and colour. Yet I always refer to mine as "my little Mexican", because Mexico was indeed its homeland until it was introduced into England in 1936. It must have taken easily to the cool climate, for it has been doing well in sunnier drawing- and living rooms ever since. In other, not-so-bright spots, it often struggles to maintain its original pale orange tones.

Our Shrimps always take pride of place on the west- and south-facing window-sills where there is abundant light all the year round. Once one has discovered and assessed the almost perfect position for a specimen it is additionally attractive if your plant's colour merges with the surroundings. For example my lounge, except for the white walls,

**Beloperone guttata**

is a mixture of autumn colours — golds, browns, oranges — and this little fellow always looks as if he was designed to live in that room.

The Shrimp needs warmth of between 50° and 60°F (10° and 15.5°C). A pot-bound specimen should be re-potted in the spring into a slightly larger pot containing J.I.P. No. 3, and regular manuring is very important. Many of the finest ones are treated somewhat drastically by fairly severe pruning, and the bracts of particularly weak or very young plants are continually removed until a sturdy plant has been developed. Then, all one has to worry about is over-watering, or splashing the bracts, which will cause a horrid discolouration of the foliage or the "shrimps".

# Billbergia nutans

*Angel's Tears*

This bromeliad — the Angel's Tears — is the best known

of the family, and was named in honour of the Swedish botanist J. G. Billberg, who lived during the eighteenth and early nineteenth centuries. Unlike most of its large family, it has no central rosette or cup in which to collect water, but being a terrestrial plant it will grow quite happily in an ordinary flower-pot containing a standard houseplant compost, and this should be watered whenever the top compost becomes dry.

So often, such prettily coloured plants have strong likes and dislikes which sometimes make them difficult subjects to care for. Yet the Angel's Tears, with its bright pink bracts and greenish-violet blooms, which hang so gracefully like a collection of tears, needs very little attention, and should not prove troublesome even for a beginner. It is strange to think that this native of warm countries like Brazil, Paraguay and Argentina can grow so well in temperatures of between 50° and 60°F (10° and 15.5°C) yet it does, and quite quickly too. New plants may be propagated either by division of very large mature specimens, or from offshoots

**Billbergia nutans**

which appear at the base of the mother plant. Once potted individually, they will in turn grow at a healthy rate, and will probably need re-potting every other year. The Angel's Tears may be left outside during the summer months, but whether it remains in the home or not, a semi-shaded position is absolutely vital.

*Nutans* means nodding, and the flower-heads of this *Billbergia* really do that, especially when displayed high up in a hanging container where the delicate blooms — which unfortunately do not last very long — can be viewed to perfection. A lover of humidity, it appreciates a light syringing with luke-warm water whenever possible, but if this is not always convenient, there are various other methods of providing a constant source of humidity, as you will see on pages 14–15.

# Callistemon

## *Bottle-brush Tree*

Any bare corner which is bright and sunny can be filled to perfection with the Callistemon. Although it is no rarity, it is unfortunately seen only occasionally, despite the fact that it is easy to care for. Called "Bottle-brush Plants", obviously because of their weird flower formation, the spiky blooms really do resemble this useful domestic brush — or would do if brushes varied from an orange to a vivid red! This family of twenty-five evergreen shrubs may be found in Australia and New Caledonia, and those in cultivation make marvellous houseplants. Now that dwarfing chemicals have taken a hand in restricting their natural growth, they have been rendered more easily saleable, and certainly more suitable for those of us with smallish rooms. Yet, they have retained their diverse roles,

**151**

serving excellently as decorative shrubs on a cool verandah or balcony during the warmer months, whereas for the remainder of the year they will be quite at home in a conservatory or greenhouse at a temperature between 45° and 50°F (7° and 10°C) — and even the youngest specimens bloom in the middle of each year!

## Callistemon

In my experience of Bottle-brush Plants, they definitely grow better when pot-bound, but this does not mean that once you have purchased your specimen you can forget about it. In the spring of every third year they must be re-potted into fresh J.I.P. No. 3 compost, and re-housed in a container which just snugly holds the root-ball. Then, at the beginning of each of the following two years, about an inch or so of the old top-soil should be removed, and the pot topped-up with a new supply.

In the growing period, water should be fed to them

freely whenever the damp compost starts to become dry. Although the quantity must be greatly reduced in the cooler seasons the compost must never be allowed to become so parched that the roots themselves dry out.

Particularly when it is hot, a close inspection of all your plants for pests should be a daily routine, but with the Callistemon, which is relatively bug-free, you do not have to worry quite so much.

# Camellia japonica

## *Common Camellia*

I consider the Camellia family to be a real godsend for it gives us not only the rich evergreen shrubs with gorgeous single and double blooms, but also — and this may surprise you — the leaves of the *Camellia sinensis*, better known, when infused, as China tea. For centuries, all types of Camellias have been cultivated by the Japanese and Chinese, and are often to be found growing in shrubland at altitudes of up to 9,000 feet. It was from East Asia that they were first introduced into Europe in 1739. This was mainly as a result of the studies of Georg Josef Kamel, after whom the Camellia was named. Kamel was a Jesuit pharmacist, who wrote and published papers on these species in the early 1700s in the Philippines.

Whether grown in the garden or in tubs, Camellias are lime-haters and so your soil should be acidic, with equal proportions of leafmould, peat, loam and sand. Avoid hard tap-water for soft lime-free water or, better still, rainwater is much better. Never allow the roots to become too dry, or premature dropping of the flower buds will occur. Keep the compost moist and syringe the foliage at the same

**Camellia japonica**

time, and as often as you are able, for Camellias love plenty of damp, see pages 14–15.

They also benefit enormously when left outside during the warmer months, although some protection from the direct sun is necessary. Camellias make good pot plants, and will live happily in a light but coolish room, and those in an east or north-facing window will take as much light as you are able to give them.

Summer feeding with a slow-acting organic fertiliser works wonders, and when frosts threaten the full blooms, cover larger plants with close netting, and bring smaller specimens indoors for the night.

# Campanula

*Star of Bethlehem, Italian Bellflower*

This elegant trailer has no connection with Bethlehem at all! In fact, both the popular and Latin names refer only to the star-like blooms, which are available in white (*Cam-*

*panula isophylla alba*), blue (*C. isophylla*) and mauve (*C.i. mayii*). In the wild they live in a small and very rocky terrain near Genoa (where they were first discovered in 1868), and yet when grown in a pot they expect very different conditions. They like a rich compost such as J.I.P. No. 2 or 3, and ample liquid manure from April to September.

**Campanula**

Although they look lovely growing almost anywhere, their beauty is best displayed in a hanging basket where they can trail over the edges of the container for several feet, covered in their masses of little stars. Each year when deciding which particular plants will be included in my hanging gardens, I vow to have a change, but I invariably weaken and include this old favourite in at least one container.

Unfortunately, the *Campanula* is not an evergreen, and needs to be kept very dry and cool when it dies down at the beginning of the dormancy period. By February or March slightly warmer surroundings will encourage it to sprout, and as soon as this happens the compost must be kept evenly moist. The flower-heads which form at the leaf joints appear in mid-summer, and will continue blooming until the autumn, as long as there is plenty of bright indirect light, ample water, and the dead flowers are removed when they start to fade.

Make the most of your specimens each spring and replace the old compost with a fresh mixture and always prune back any unwanted and sickly shoots. New healthy three-inch cuttings may be used for propagating, and you will find that they root quickly if placed in a jar of water.

# Citrus mitis

## *Calamondin*

Anyone who enjoys eating something a bit different will certainly find the Calamondin orange tree interesting. The fruits, which are rather bitter and on the small side, may be used—if you can gather enough—to make marmalade, and I assure you it is absolutely delicious! However, if I had to choose between my stomach and the glorious sight of these miniature orange trees when flowering and fruiting, I would most certainly prefer the latter.

At first they do appear costly, but when one thinks of the time and labour involved in rearing them, and the expense of keeping nurseries heated, then one can appreciate that varieties like this are good value for money. It is always a good idea to consider costly specimens carefully before buying, for if they need a particular requirement which you cannot provide — such as a sunny siting — you should leave them alone. Otherwise, not only will your money be wasted, but you will be so disappointed that you may never give the plant another chance even in the most conducive surroundings.

**Citrus mitis**

The correct watering of the Calamondin is the biggest headache. You must use common sense, and soak the plant thoroughly when required. Then, and this is important, allow the compost to dry out before repeating the operation. During the summer you can combine watering with a regular weak dose of fertiliser, and perhaps put the plant out in a sunny part of the garden, where it can ripen nicely. However, never allow it to remain outside later than September when the first frosts are likely.

With a high humidity, fresh air, and a winter warmth of 50°F (10°C), your little orange should keep going for years.

# Clivia miniata

*Kaffir Lily, Natal Lily*

I am very grateful to the granddaughter of Clive of India, the Duchess of Northumberland, for she was the first to cultivate the Kaffir Lily. Everyone who has enjoyed the bright reddish-orange head of the lily must at times have wondered what would have happened if she had never shown any interest in this bulbous plant from South Africa. Who knows? It might have been lost to us forever, so in gratitude, the Clivia was named after her maiden name of Clive.

I receive many letters from owners who want to know why their lily shows no inclination to bloom. Although this one is a hardy and easy plant to grow, during the dormancy period it must be allowed to rest, as nature intended and it will not like you if you unwittingly encourage it to grow by feeding and watering it in abundance, and providing warm growing conditions. To ensure those lily-like heads in the spring, the opposite treatment is vital — no manuring, only a little water, and a temperature which does not exceed 55°F (13°C).

**Clivia miniata**

Often it seems to bloom more readily when confined to its original pot, but when re-potting is essential, and only after flowering is over, a one-size larger pot should be used. J.I.P. No. 3 is a suitable compost, and you can divide the plant at the same time. Your minimum-watering programme must continue until after the central stem, which supports the flower-head, makes an appearance. When it reaches a height of six inches or so, weekly manuring and plenty of bright light are vital. Although watering may also be increased, the compost must be allowed nearly to dry out in between times, otherwise rotting, which is always a danger during the non-flowering months, can easily occur.

## Guzmania lingulata

### Scarlet Star

My first *Guzmania* was purchased near the Royal Botanical Gardens at Kew, and the beautiful solitary orange-yellow bracts lasted for a considerable time before dying. Much of the excitement with this and other bromeliads lies in the fact that, even after the flower-heads fade (and being hot-house plants this may occur at almost any time of the year) there is still new life hidden in them. By keeping them almost dry throughout the dormancy period (after flowering has finished) and later increasing their watering a little at a time, small off-shoots will quickly form in between the protective "arms" of the mature outer leaves. In the first year, my original one produced seven such babies, and once they were four- to six-inches high I could have re-potted them separately in a mixture of sharp sand, leafmould, sphagnum moss and J.I.P. No. 2; I did not, however, tear them away from the parental home, because they frequently do better when left alone. The adult plant should be cut down to as near soil level as possible, without damaging the offshoots, and the second generation can be left to grow into a fine group of flowering plants the following year.

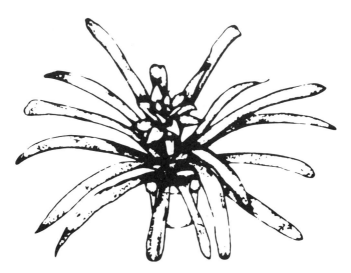

**Guzmania lingulata**

From Central and South America, the *Guzmania* was named after the eighteenth-century Spanish naturalist Anastasio Guzman. A good, filtered light in a normally heated room suits the Scarlet Star very well, with daily syringing of the foliage to keep it dust-free, and also to raise the humidity (see pages 14–15). The central cup-like urn must be kept topped-up with luke-warm water, rainwater if possible. Most plants seem to prefer rainwater, and even a light summer shower should never be allowed to pass without the Scarlet Star benefiting from this naturally-soft moisture.

Each plant blooms only once in its lifetime, but do not let this perturb you for the rewards are far greater than the work entailed in caring for this undemanding epiphyte.

# Hibiscus rosa-sinensis

*Rose of China, Rose Mallow, Chinese Rose*

To the ladies of the islands of Tahiti in the Pacific, this beautiful flowering shrub has a relevant part to play in their lives. Not only does it serve as a colourful reddish-pink ornament in the hair and dress, but when worn by a young woman, it tells admirers that she is neither engaged nor married, and is therefore free to receive their attentions.

At first, one might think that these blossoms are a bitter disappointment, because they only last a day before dying. However, this feeling is quickly dispelled by the quantity of them which abound almost continuously throught the summer months. To have any luck with this rose from China, a constantly moist growing mixture of J.I.P. No. 3 and coarse sand is vital throughout the growing months, and so is a temperature of between 55° and 65°F (13° and 18°C). Try to keep the level as static as possible, for although a difference of ten degrees will not really harm it, constant fluctuations will encourage the flowers to fall whilst still in bud.

**Hibiscus rosa-sinensis**

Introduced into Europe as long ago as 1731, the species is also known as Shoe Black, and Shoe Flower in Jamaica, where the petals of the large five-inch blooms are used to polish shoes! What a sacrilege! There are a number of strains available in single or double blooms of cream, red, rose pink, pale yellow, rich crimson, yellow and purple, and white and red. But for my money, the original reddish-pink, which is grown outside on terraces and balconies, and is wintered under cover or reared indoors, certainly takes some beating.

A light spot and regular feeding completes their summer care, and in winter they can either be watered in reduced quantities, or kept entirely dry until the following spring.

# Hoya

## *Wax Flowers*

The two Wax Flowers you are most likely to meet are the *H. bella* (the Small Wax Flower), and the larger-blooming *H. carnosa*. The latter one can be found growing in the wilds of China and Australia, and in the home may reach a height of ten feet or so, if given ample space and good growing conditions! The *H. bella*, which has smaller sweet-smelling flowers, looks best when incorporated in a hanging basket or wall display. Then the clusters of delicate white star-shaped blooms, with their reddish-purple centres, can be seen at eye-level to greater advantage.

It is a succulent, and originally came from India. Like the *carnosa*, it needs only small quantities of water even during the flower-producing months. A daily sprinkling of tepid water over the waxy foliage will be fine. The *H. bella* likes a temperature of 65°F (18°C), unlike the *carnosa* which prefers cooler conditions of between 55° and 60°F

(13° and 15.5°C). Neither appreciates being moved about, nor even turned to ensure a more even growth, quickly showing their displeasure by dropping many of their blooms. So try to leave them undisturbed in a bright position away from the sun — a protected part of a sun-lounge or greenhouse would be perfect.

The *carnosa* is in its element when displayed as a climber, and a firm support around which to twine its long stems is essential. Unlike most flowering plants, once its flowers die they should be left so that new blooms can form in their place. Any cuttings — which must be taken after blooming is over — may be rooted in a moist and sandy compost. Later they can be re-potted, four or five to a pot containing a light and open blend of two parts of leafmould to one part of sharp sand. (For sterilising compost, see page 17.) We call these flowering evergreens, and they take their name from Thomas Hoy who was head gardener to the Duke of Northumberland during the eighteenth century, at Syon House in Middlesex.

**Hoya**

# Hypocyrta glabra

*Clog Plant*

Every day my plants give me so much pleasure. I still marvel at their willingness to survive under the most alien conditions.

Clog Plants are one such example, and in their native tropical South America they live high up in the trees of the rain forests, where the conditions are humid and hot. You might assume that similar conditions would have to prevail in the home before you could begin to cultivate these charming foreigners, but it does not always work out like that. The Clog certainly thrives better when surrounded by a moist atmosphere (see pages 14–15), but it will grow reasonably well in an ordinary home

**Hypocyrta glabra**

environment. Excessive watering is not required and during the summer it will enjoy being treated in the same way as all your other varieties. With its fleshy little leaves it can easily withstand fairly dry conditions in the cooler months, only requiring the occasional drink and a warmth of about 60°F (15.5°C) is just right. It needs only a little attention, which makes it an ideal subject for those who do not have much time on their hands.

The beauty of these trailing plants lies in their blooms, which, although fairly small, last for a long time. They are pouched and tubular-shaped flowers, which appear each summer from the leaf axils, and are at first a vivid reddish-orange, but as the plants age so the flowers become more scarlet in colour.

Each spring any untidy growth should be cut back vigorously, and three-inch cuttings will sometimes oblige by rooting in a coarse, sandy compost. Do not postpone your pruning until the flowering period is over because blooms will only form on the new year's shoots and so will be totally unaffected by your snipping!

# Impatiens

## *Busy Lizzie*

As far as flowering plants are concerned, the "Busy Lizzie" is one of the best values for money today, and I am not only thinking of those pot plants from the florist's which are covered with non-stop splashes of colour from the middle of spring to late autumn, and sometimes in the winter too. For those of you wishing to fill a flower-bed, or a number of window boxes with the maximum variety of colour and inexpensively, there is probably no better choice.

Sowing a single packet of seeds in the early spring, in trays of seed compost, will give you as many plants as you need, and probably more besides to display in tubs and hanging baskets as well. These tropical African plants which have been with us for nearly a hundred years can indeed be set almost anywhere where there is a light sunny

**Impatiens**

position, and with the colours varying from white to numerous shades of pink, orange, red and lilac, they make a simple yet brilliant showpiece.

Two-to-three-inch cuttings will quickly produce roots when placed in a glass of water. Then, for indoor planting, pot them in J.I.P. No. 2, and to produce the best results with thick and bushy growth plant three or four cuttings to each pot. You can pinch out some of the top shoots as they appear.

Planting out on a larger scale requires a peaty or sandy garden loam which is quick to drain, and whether you have hundreds outside or a solitary one indoors, all will need frequent watering especially if the summer proves to be a real scorcher! Then, a thorough drenching early in the morning and again in the evening should prove adequate, and will also discourage "red spider" which hates moisture. Any attacks from this unwanted visitor can be treated effectively with several thorough sprayings of liquid Derris, not missing the undersides of the leaves.

The "spider" is always encouraged when the temperature is hot and dry, so to provide more humidity indoors see pages 14–15.

# Jasminum polyanthum

### *Chinese Jasmine*

Whenever I think of Jasmine, my thoughts tend not to stray to this fragrant white flowering plant but instead to linger on the memory of a Persian garden. Many of my friends live in that ancient, beautiful country, and the name *Jasminum* comes from the Persian-Arabic *yasmin* — an enchanting girl's name meaning "white flower".

**Jasminum polyanthum**

The Common White Jasmine (*J. officinale*) was first brought from Persia as long ago as 1548, but the Chinese Jasmine is a relative newcomer (1891), though it is now a firmly established variety. This one is happiest in coolish surroundings, so you can use a bright, unheated room where temperatures do not exceed 55°F (13°C) in winter or 60°F (15.5°C) during the summer. The Jasmine will grow far better, however, when placed outside during the warm months where a free flow of fresh air and a good light are in abundance.

Once flowering is over, and after pruning, re-pot your specimen into a one-size larger pot, using a mixture of well-rotted humus and enough sand to make the compost open and porous (for sterilising compost, see page 17). Alternatively, J.I.P. No. 2 or 3 may be used on their own, and remember to put a cane or wire loop in the pot, so that the new shoots have something on which to climb. Growth will be rampant, and it is well to take cuttings each July so that, once the older specimen is past its best, it can easily be replaced, and stock increased with already established ones. In the early autumn, before the first frosts, potted plants must be brought indoors and kept very dry. When spring comes, watering can be slowly increased, but even in the hottest months the soil must be allowed to dry out in between waterings.

# Nerium oleander

*Oleander, Rose Bay*

When I look at our own Oleanders, which grow in tubs around the patio area of our home, I still find it very difficult to believe that these lovely evergreen shrubs could be harmful. With their greyish, leathery leaves, and handsome flower-heads of white, red, peach, pink and yellow they look so innocent, and make such a stunning show of colour. But do not let this mislead you, for beautiful as these plants undoubtedly are, they should be treated with the utmost respect.

Always keep them well away from young children because they are extremely poisonous, and men have been known to die from consuming hot drinks which have been stirred with an Oleander twig. However, there is no need to be frightened of them. In the summer, once flowering has ceased, the Oleander will need pruning. Just remember to wash your hands thoroughly afterwards.

**Nerium oleander**

Five- or six-inch cuttings taken in late spring will root fairly well in a container of water, and then can be potted up in a standard potting compost. They are extremely well-liked plants, particularly in warmer climates such as the Mediterranean countries where they grow out-of-doors, but in Britain the weather is far too severe in the colder months, and they need frost-free shelter. High temperatures and artificial forms of heating are certainly frowned upon, and a coolish room of 50°–55°F (10°–13°C) is much preferred. During the dormancy period the plant will need little moisture, but when new growth appears, watering should be increased until it is in good supply.

To encourage your Oleander to bloom, which is sometimes difficult, provide it with lots of sunshine, which will mean keeping it outside on a window-ledge, balcony or in the garden throughout the summer. Give it regular doses of fertiliser, and possibly two waterings a day, not forgetting overhead spraying of the foliage, and you will almost certainly guarantee the blossoms!

# Passiflora caerulea

## *Passion Flower*

The Passion Flower was introduced into Europe from South Brazil in 1699. The name *Passiflora* was first bestowed on this flower by early Spanish missionaries and friars in tropical America, because in it they saw the perfect representation of the crucifixion of Christ, and used the flower-head to teach and convert the inhabitants. The five anthers represented the five woulds received by Christ, whilst the three styles were the three nails used for each of his hands and feet. In the central part of the bloom one can see the sign of the Cross, the stalk of the stamen resembles the crown of thorns, and the ten petals represent Christ's apostles. No more perfect flower could have been found to explain those historic and religious events so aptly; the blue and white blooms themselves are a work of art!

The plant may be grown in milder and more temperate climates outside on balconies and terraces, but a frost-free

**Passiflora caerulea**

conservatory or greenhouse is by far the best. As a true houseplant it will need good conditions to grow really well, but none of its requirements are impossible, or even difficult. Normally at their best when restricted to a smallish pot, they must be fed, watered and sprayed very generously throughout the summer, and a warm, light siting at about 65°F (18°C) will encourage the buds to open.

Enthusiasts who leave their potted specimens outside in the garden must bring them indoors again in early October, to a minimum temperature of 50°F (10°C). Then they will need far less water, and later they will drop their leaves.

Spring should see the pruning back of old weak growth, and after re-potting in a mixture of leafmould, J.I.P. No. 2, with enough sand to make it porous, new luxuriant

171

foliage will soon become evident. When it does, from the summer onwards, it will frame those gorgeous seven-inch blossoms beautifully.

# Regal pelargoniums

Frequently we think of Pelargoniums as being suitable for growing only out-of-doors in tubs, window boxes and hanging baskets, but there is one particular variety known as the *Pelargonium x domesticum* which also provides a gorgeous show when reared in the home. In Britain they are more commonly referred to as "Regal" or "Fancy" Pelargoniums, whilst in the U.S.A. they are better known as "Martha Washington" or "U.S. Show" Pelargoniums.

There are in excess of one thousand strains in cultivation today, covering almost every conceivable colour and tone, and some particularly beautiful ones include "Aztec", a two-toned red and purple flowering strain, the "Muriel Hawkins", the white-flowering blooms of which are splashed with red, the mauve and red blooming "Rhodamine", and the pink-headed "Delight". Then there is "Pandora" with its flowers of brilliant red, the exquisite pink and white "Godfrey's Pride" as well as the "Black Knight", the reddish-purple petals of which are edged with white.

Cuttings can be taken any time from late February or early March to the end of September. A number of tip cuttings, three- to four-inches long, are severed just above a leaf joint, using a very sharp knife or razor blade. Then each cutting is trimmed so that the cut stem terminates immediately below a leaf axil, for it is only from these joints that roots will form. (If this unwanted length of stem below the joint is allowed to remain, it will rot, possibly adversely affecting the growing plant later on). The cuttings are lightly dusted with a fungicidal rooting powder before setting them in shallow pots containing a damp mixture of equal parts of J.I.P. No. 1 and sand. They need a light position either in a greenhouse, conservatory or on a warm sunless window-sill, but whilst they are rooting they should be lightly covered with newspaper. Spraying the leaves lightly with water will help to keep the cuttings fresh, and encourage rooting, but the compost must never be wetter than moist otherwise all sorts of problems may occur such as Black Leg, Grey Mould and Black Root Rot.

**Regal pelargonium**

Unfortunately, Black Leg lives up to its name by causing the once firm stems to soften and turn black, and the bacteria concerned is encouraged by over-cold and wet cultivating conditions, especially where unsterilised soil has been used. The only really effective means of preventing this and other diseases is to ensure that one follows a strict code of hygiene.

Several rooted cuttings should be transferred to a four-inch flower-pot containing an open mixture of two parts of J.I.P. No. 2 and one part of sand. Water fairly freely throughout the growing months, and from May to September introduce a weak dose of liquid fertiliser such as Phostrogen, every ten days or so. The larger and more established specimens do particularly well when this Phostrogen feed is alternated with one of the branded liquid tomato fertilisers, and a safe dosage to use is one of approximately half the strength recommended on the bottle. Plenty of bright sunless light and fresh air is an integral part of their successful cultivation, but once flowering ceases, watering should be reduced and the plants pruned back to within six- or seven-inches of the compost. These pieces, thus severed, can be used to propagate more new plants, but when this exercise is performed late in the year the cuttings, once rooted, should remain where they are until the spring. Even if they become somewhat "leggy" in the process it matters little, for all young plants should be stopped or cut back around April to encourage a strong and bushy growth.

Over-wintering Pelargoniums is easy enough as long as one remembers that whilst room temperatures are low the compost must be kept quite dry. Specimens living in a warm environment in excess of 60°F (15.5°C) will naturally need a little water to keep them happy.

# Rosa chinensis minima

*Miniature Rose*

Generally speaking, roses play such a small part in indoor gardening that I had no intention of including any in these pages at all, but I recently saw a houseplant section in one of a chain of well-known stores, and scurried inside.

The counter was fairly well-stocked with a variety of foliage and flowering plants, and in the ten or so minutes I was browsing several women purchased some blooming miniature roses. The pots carried no advice tags at all and I wondered how these poor, delicate-looking roses would fare whilst the owners were experimenting to find the right treatment for them. I hope that perhaps some of these snippets of advice may help you.

There are several forms of miniature rose but they all require the same cool surroundings in the resting period, and if there is no unheated room in the house put them in a shed or in the garden. If, however, they are not plunged into the soil with their pots, they must be brought in at the first signs of frost.

**Rosa chinesis minima**

Keep them on the dry side until about February and after re-potting them in fresh compost, watering must be slowly increased. All old wood should be cut away before moving them into light, warmer conditions. Once the growth is well under way, and the buds are starting to form, begin feeding regularly with a suitable fertiliser, and continue it until the early autumn.

These miniatures may look tiny and fragile but they are much tougher than they look and can always be transferred to the garden if you get tired of them. Once you have one, however, this is highly unlikely.

# Saintpaulia

## *African Violet*

Surely this is the most popular of all houseplants, and no wonder! During the year one has a low-growing, decorative foliage plant, and in the summer months it will be adorned with a multitude of blooms ranging from white to various shades of pink, red, lilac and mauve.

I occasionally receive a letter about a *Saintpaulia* which shows no inclination to flower, and this failure is frequently due to inadequate light. This may partly be the fault of horticultural scribes who say they need a semi-shaded siting. This is true in a way — for Saintpaulias should not be subjected to harmful rays of the summer sun, but bright indirect light is a must to ensure blooming. For both flat and house dwellers, I always advocate, from May to September, a daily stint outside on an east-facing window-sill where the right kind of light is available. Not only will specimens flower, but with all that fresh air they will take on a more healthy appearance altogether. Another good thing is to alternate fertilisers which should be given during the growing months. By comparing the constituent qualities of nitrogen (leaf maker) and potash ($K_2O$, flower maker), not forgetting the phosphates ($P_2O_5$) for root making, you can decide upon a good balanced diet. My mixed collection enjoys one of two blends every alternate feed, and it certainly benefits from a change of menu!

**Saintpaulia**

These bushy plants, which grow as high up as 3,000 feet above sea level, take their name from the German who first discovered them in tropical East Africa — Baron Walter von Saint Paul-Illaire.

Propagating from leaf-cuttings is found by many to be unusually difficult, so try placing the stem, with the leaf attached, in a glass of water. Given time, roots will form, and then the cutting may be potted in equal parts of J.I.P. No. 2 and sphagnum moss.

# Schlumbergera

*Christmas Cactus*

I think the "in-built" calendar which tells the Schlumbergera to flower must have gone very much awry last year because instead of flowering, as is usual, around Christmas time mine waited until about March before it formed any buds at all, and I noticed that many other specimens were doing exactly the same thing. Often better known as the "Zygocactus", the Schlumbergera is one of the easiest indoor plants to grow and its flowers, which are trumpet-shaped and somewhat resemble a fuchsia, are available in a selection of pinks and reds.

Occasionally, however, the flowers can prove somewhat of a disappointment when they fall whilst still in very tight bud, and a variety of "wrongs" may be contributing factors. Sudden variation in light, watering and, more frequently, room temperature can well be the cause. Originally hailing from Brazil, the Christmas Cactus most enjoys a light position in a room which affords a fairly constant temperature of between 55° and 65°F (13° and 18°C) — I have mine along some south-easterly-facing French windows.

**Schlumbergera**

A short while ago I was quite surprised to see a fairly large specimen situated in a decidedly dark part of a north-facing drawing room. The owner wanted some advice about it because the pads, in their attempt to find some good light, were stretching out and had consequently become extremely long, thin and spindly. Apparently my bachelor friend had been informed by his sister that this particular specimen was the ideal type for a very dull corner, but unfortunately this is just not so. It will derive a lot of benefit from being placed outside on a well-lit window-sill, where there is some protection from the sun during the summer months, and the same principles of good light and fresh air also apply on any mild winter days.

Throughout the blooming period the compost should be kept nicely moist, but afterwards watering must be greatly reduced. This attractive cactus can be readily propagated at almost any time of the year by removing several of the jointed pads and planting them in a damp, peaty compost. Then, once they have rooted they should be re-potted individually in three-inch pots containing a mixture of one part of J.I.P. No. 1, two parts of coarse sand and two parts of crushed brick.

# Stephanotis floribunda

*Wax Flower, Madagascar Jasmine*

Unlike the Saintpaulia, the Stephanotis has never become a best-seller, no doubt because it has always been considered essentially a hot-house plant. But now, as more and more people have central heating installed, and gardening enthusiasts regard heated greenhouses as an essential rather than a luxury, the Stephanotis' chances in the popularity stakes can only be enhanced.

The fragrant clusters of white bell-shaped blooms, which

used only to be known by their inclusion in wedding bouquets, look far more lovely when seen hanging from the twining stems of a potted specimen. Like all climbers they need some support and where space is limited, a wire hoop should be adequate. For the best results the Wax Flower likes a moist atmosphere (see pages 14–15), with daily overhead syringing in a bright but sunless room. A winter temperature of between 50° and 60°F (10° and 15.5°C) should be maintained, but in the hotter months this will certainly be 10°F (5°C) higher. Careful watering is most important. Err on the dry side throughout the winter — barely damp is about right — whilst the leaf-making months should see a moist but never saturated compost. Unless you want a towering specimen, feed yours only occasionally, and keep it within the bonds of a smallish pot. Otherwise, re-pot it every other year in a slightly larger pot of J.I.P. No. 3, and watch it take off!

**Stephanotis floribunda**

Do not, however, allow it to run amok, and remove any old or damaged branches in the spring. With a bottom heat of 85°F (29°C), cuttings will root easily in a sandy compost, and when they are ready, plant several together and you will have a really lush climber!

Some specimens show a reluctance to bloom but by improving the lighting facilities and alternating between two fertilisers — one of which should contain a higher proportion of potash — this problem can be quickly rectified.

# Strelitzia reginae

*Bird of Paradise*

When selecting plants for this book I originally discarded thoughts of including this truly magnificent specimen, the Bird of Paradise, although it is a stunning example of the

**Strelitzia reginae**

work of Mother Nature. Why the indecision? Simply because, when grown from seed, these plants take between three and five years to flower, and at first I thought that no-one who was not a houseplant fanatic would be interested. Still I have hoped, and oh, how I have tried, to make these pages interesting for everyone, so I have relented and, with great pleasure, present to those who have a greenhouse, plenty of patience and time to spare, the exquisite *Strelitzia reginae*!

Even if you have none of these virtues or luxuries, next time you visit a botantical garden look out for its unmistakeable head, which is like the crest of some exotic and highly-coloured eastern bird. It is comprised of three orange and three blue petals, which are encased in a greenish-pink sheath before they finally emerge. In their native Cape Province, where the plants reach a height of four feet or so, they grow along the river banks and coastlines, and are believed to be pollinated by the sugar-birds. In the hope of reaching the nectar below the birds alight on the petals which then lever out the anthers, and these brush against the birds' breasts, depositing the pollen and almost guaranteeing the continuity of the species.

Named after, and certainly complimenting, George III's rather plain Queen Charlotte of Mecklenburg-Strelitz, the Bird of Paradise is very popular with florists, although their prices certainly would not endear them to me!

You can propagate either by division or seed; the latter method requires a warmth of 70°F (21°C) for germination. When repotting becomes necessary, a mixture of manure, rich loam, peat and sand, and a temperature of 60°F (15.5°C) is sufficient. Once summer approaches, plenty of watering, with regular manuring and protection against strong sunlight is very important.

# Streptocarpus

*Cape Primrose, Cape Cowslip*

Frequently the Cape Primrose is discarded by the beginner when flowering has ceased, probably because he knows no better — yet the more experienced enthusiast may keep his specimens from one year to the next.

**Streptocarpus**

Many of the varieties we see today are hybrids, and very lovely they are too. The *Streptocarpus rexii* Constant Nymph, for example, produces an abundance of attractive bluish-purple flowers over a very long period — from April to September — and it is no wonder that this particular one made a name for itself as a houseplant in Holland long before it became popular in Britain. One of its parents, the *S.r.* Merton Blue, also has bluish-purple blooms, but unlike the tubular heads of the offspring they are more trumpet-shaped. Now other hybrids are available in white and various shades of pink, cerise and blue, and anyone who enjoys decorative petals will certainly appreciate the frilled blooms of *S.r.* Wiesmoor Hybrids.

The *Streptocarpus* family is indigenous to South Africa and South East Asia, and can be found growing several thousand feet up amongst craggy rocks and granite boulders. So, with only limited roots, the Cape Primrose does best in a well-crocked and shallow pot and, having no tubers on which to over-winter, needs some water but in only very small quantities.

In the spring and summer it should be manured regularly, and have enough water to keep the compost damp. It may be propagated from either seed or leaf-cuttings. The latter method entails cutting the leaf down the centre and then planting the two halves, or sections of them, in a peat compost with the knife-cut downwards. Soon lots of tiny plantlets will appear and once these are big enough they may be potted in a standard compost which is light and crumbly to the touch.

These plants may originate in hotter climates than our own but do not let this fool you for, although they need a light spot, make sure they are protected from the sun.

# Tillandsia

Tillandsias are a wonderful example of how perfectly nature equips plants to withstand extreme conditions. The Spanish Moss or Old Man's Beard (*Tillandsia usneoides*) immediately springs to mind. Perhaps not a very prepossessing-looking plant with its long twisting silvery threads but even this one has a built-in food supply, and does not require a sure footing to thrive. All it needs is a light support, and in its native tropical South America a tree or even a cable-wire is often its home. Its lifeline is plenty of humidity, which the absorbent scales of the stems soak up, and as these fill out so the long shoots become greener. Birds regard these as ideal nesting material and unwittingly spread and propagate the plants on their homeward journey.

The Blue Torch (*Tillandsia linderiana*) is different, having beautifully designed bracts which look almost flat. This variety is more typical of the type as a whole, for it is the rosettes of leaves which act as a water-storing vessel.

**Tillandsia**

All are fairly easy to care for and will grow well once the root-ball is wrapped in damp sphagnum moss. Place some cork-bark round the moss and secure with wire — preferably covered with plastic — to contain the whole. They must have plenty of humidity and how to supply this adequately is dealt with in detail on pages 14–15. The compost should always be just moist and, with a shaded position in a temperature of 55°-60°F (13°-15°C), you should be able safely to forget them — until they start to flower.

The Spanish Moss grows yellowish-green flowers, whilst the torch-like and rosy pink bracts of the Blue Torch develop lovely bluish-purple blooms. They are very long lasting and are so delicate and colourful and almost unreal that they look like something out of a fairy story!

# Vinca rosea

## *Madagascar Periwinkle*

The Madagascar Periwinkle was first discovered over two hundred years ago by the French, who took it to Paris in 1756. It was not long before it came to England and in 1757 it made its first appearance at Chelsea. In medicine today, extracts of the plant are used in the treatment of diabetes and certain forms of cancer. A long-established background indeed for a very fine specimen.

It is still widespread in the tropics where it blooms at almost any time of the year, but in colder climes flowering is usually restricted to the summer and autumn.

Then the adult Periwinkle, a bushy plant between one and two feet high, bears a single flattish flower at the tip of each shoot. About an inch across, the blooms vary in colour from a rose-pink to a pure white face with a small red eye. This is a little beauty — it is far more pleasing to look at than its near-relative, the Hardy Periwinkle (*Vinca major*), and is very much the indoor type.

The Madagascar bloomer is not all that difficult to cope with in temperatures of around 50°F (10°C). One of the main requirements is a very humid atmosphere (see page 17), which can be augmented by a daily all-over showering with warmish water and this may sometimes be extended to include the compost, before there is any likelihood of it drying out.

**Vinca rosea**

After the flowers have died, the straggly-looking remains may be cut back leaving just over one-third of the original growth, and the plant should be kept on the dry side. In February or March it can be transferred to a bigger pot containing a light compost such as J.I.P. No. 2 and when shoots are observed, watering may be increased. Once the growth is doing well, increase your stock by rooting two or three inch cuttings in sand, at 65°F (18°C).

# Vriesia splendens

*Flaming Sword*

Splendid, showy — the Flaming Sword lives up to these adjectives and more. Although it is the sword-shaped red bracts with yellow flowers at which we marvel most, the strap-like bluish-green leaves, banded with a purplish-brown are also worthy of our admiration. As the bract emerges like some long blood-stained rapier from the centre of the rosette, the foliage begins to lose its distinct markings but even then it remains a lovely shade of deep green.

**Vriesia splendens**

The bracts last for some time, no doubt making up for the fact that their appearance is a solo effort. Each specimen blooms only once in its lifetime but this does not mean that once the flower-heads fade the plant has lost its usefulness. The Flaming Sword, like many brome-liads, will start to produce offshoots round the base of the adult plant when the flowering period is in progress. After blooming, both the head and leaves of the original specimen will die back.

Once the offshoots are six or more inches high they may be carefully removed with their roots and re-potted individually into small holders containing an equal mixture of chopped peat-moss (or sand) and well-rotted leafmould. These are fairly slow-growers and will take about four years to reach maturity and produce their glorious blossom.

These plants grow better when their roots are cosily housed in a pot which is relatively small for their height, neither squashing nor providing them with lots of space.

A native of Guyana, the *Vriesia* requires shaded but good light in a warm room, and the compost, although moist, must never be waterlogged.

# CHAPTER
# THIRTEEN

# Flowering Plants — not so easy

## Acalypha hispida

*Chenille Plant, Red-Hot Cat's Tail*

I have never seen a photograph or sketch which does this plant justice, but take it from me, a show of these Chenille Plants can be absolutely breathtaking.

**Acalypha hispida**

They are demanding and need copious quantities of warm and damp air, which they have in the jungles of New

Guinea where they were originally found. Temperatures of around 65°–70°F (18°–21°C) must be combined with frequent spraying and this treatment must continue, even after the brilliant red catkins appear, although from then on it must be limited to the foliage itself. Other methods of avoiding dry-air damage are mentioned on pages 14–15. Any shaded conservatory which boasts a fountain, however small, will be an ideal setting for them. I once knew a keen grower who produced some beautiful specimens which he kept in his fairly larger shower-room, and as he was a frequent bather, the plants probably believed that they were still in their steamy forest! They are happy surrounded by moist air and they also like their compost to be kept moist with tepid water.

When the winter comes, manuring must be suspended until the spring and then the plant will benefit from a light trimming and new compost. A mixture of J.I.P. No. 1 and peat or, alternatively, equal parts of J.I.P. No. 1, peat and well-rotted leafmould are equally good. For sterilising see page 17. Cuttings may be reared fairly easily and young three- to four-inch shoots will root well in a sandy soil, particularly with the aid of some bottom heat of around 75°F (23°C). There are a number of Acalyphas, the Lance Copperleaf (*A. godseffiana*) for instance, which are grown for their cream and green evergreen foliage, but all are particularly appetising to the red spider mite, so watch out for it!

# Anthurium

## *Tail Flower, Flamingo Flower*

Anthuriums are South American in origin. The *Anthurium scherzerianum* (Flamingo Flower or Painter's Palette) was discovered by Herr Scherzer of Vienna and introduced into Europe from Guatemala around 1880. A much smaller specimen than the two foot tall *A. andreanum* (Tail Flower) from Columbia, the *A. scherzerianum* is by far the better plant for indoor culture because it is more compact and less difficult (though not easy) to care for in the home.

Both Anthuriums require very high humidity (see page 17) in cultivation because in their natural habitat they grow between rocks and boulders where the air is moist. Like all epiphytes, they have a comparatively small root system, which in their case needs only small but frequent quantities of water, preferably rainwater. To ensure that saturation through waterlogging never occurs, the pot must be crocked with at least an inch of brick or clay pot pieces before adding the compost — a mixture of either sphagnum moss and decomposed leafmould, or equal parts of J.I.P. No. 2 and peat. For sterilising such mixtures please turn to page 17.

As the plants mature, new roots appear at the top of the compost, and these should always be covered with damp sphagnum moss. Re-potting is usually needed only every other year, but specimens which are particularly happy with their environment, and growing really well, may need a fresh mixture each spring. However, these plants do not appreciate being constantly on the move and often grow best when their roots are somewhat restricted. Suitable temperatures vary from 60°–80°F (15.5°–26°C), but any drop below the 60°F (15.5°C) minimum will probably cause the plants to take a rest until greater warmth becomes available.

A real pet in many of the Scandinavian countries where higher indoor temperatures are the norm, the Flamingo Flower loves light, and plenty of it. Always play safe an

**Anthurium**

provide some screening from the summer sun, although in the winter this will prove beneficial.

# Aphelandra

*Zebra Plant*

Many people have at some time been presented with a Zebra Plant and certainly lots of these, with their prominently veined foliage, continue to grace their surroundings. However, there are owners who turf these potted plants out as soon as the yellow flower-heads die which is not only a little heartless but totally unnecessary. Even after blooming, and possibly the loss of many lower leaves as well, a sad-looking, flowerless and top-heavy specimen may be improved with a little loving patience on your part.

Anyone with a propagator may rear lots of new plants by first removing the dead flower-spike cleanly with a knife. Then one has to wait patiently for a pair of leaves to develop from the top of the leaf joints. Once these arc

**193**

**Aphelandra**

large enough to handle they, too, should be severed with about half an inch of stem attached, potted in a peaty compost, and placed in a warm propagator. This, however, is not always very practical but no special equipment is needed to air-layer a plant; indeed anyone can achieve some success with care. Air-layering is a simple but effective method which produces two compact plants from the original one and is particularly suitable for those leafless leggy wonders we have already mentioned. For more detailed information see page 29.

Successful keepers of Aphelandras would argue that leaf-dropping problems are really the owner's fault in the first instance, and to a great extent this is so. Regularly watering the compost with luke-warm water so that it does not get an opportunity to dry out during the growing period will certainly help to avoid any trouble, as will a daily syringing of the foliage.

The Zebra comes from Brazil and Mexico, and hates a hot, sunny or dry atmosphere, so provide the opposite, namely a comfortable warmth of 60°F (15.5°C) in a lightly shaded spot with a very moist atmosphere, see pages 14–15.

# Ardisia crispa

## *Coral Berry*

We do not see these naturally slow-growing shrubs as often as we would like and even when they are occasionally offered for sale, covered with a multitude of brilliant red berries, they always seem to be somewhat costly. If the clock is not your enemy, and you are more than happy to wait three years for your plant to bear fruit, germinating the "Coral Berry" from seed in the spring is obviously the solution.

The East Indies is where this most interesting subject comes from and it likes the warmth and damp of its homeland. You can make it feel happy in an atmosphere at about 60°F (15.5°C) which can be made ideally humid by spraying the foliage with luke-warm water every morning and evening. This treatment will also help to prevent the fruits shrivelling and falling prematurely. When the flowers are in evidence, the spraying must be discontinued and so other methods of providing humidity have to be practised. For some of these see pages 14–15.

Ordinary watering, with an occasional dose of fertiliser, is all that is required during the growing season and only in the hottest months will they need any shielding from the sun. That is if they are in a south- or west-facing window, for anywhere else they should be given full light at all times.

Once the berries are past their best, the branches should be pruned nearly half-way down, whereupon they will sprout new growth. When that happens retain the two

**Ardisia crispa**

strongest shoots and remove the others. Re-pot those which obviously need it into a one-size larger pot, using a compost such as J.I.P. No. 3 or, alternatively, for those who like to mix their own, equal parts of loam, well-rotted manure, peat and coarse sand. (The sterilising of such mixture is dealt with on page 17). Throughout the winter they may be kept on the dry side in cool surroundings but in neither winter nor summer must they be subjected to any kind of draught.

# Clianthus

*Glory Pea, Parrot Bill*

Both varieties of Clianthus look really magnificent when in bloom and both will tax the skills of even the most experienced gardeners. However, success can be achieved and a challenge can prove exciting and stimulating for the best of us. Anyway, with such exotic names as the Glory Pea, the Parrot Bill, the Kaka Beak and the Lobster Claw, how could anyone with imagination and a heated greenhouse resist the temptation to try to raise the flowers to which these fascinating names refer? Coloured a brilliant scarlet, the three-to four-inch long blooms hang in clusters, and indeed look very much like the claws of a lobster.

**Clianthus**

The Glory Pea (*Clianthus formosus- syn. C. dampieri*) may be found growing wild in Australia but, sad to say, it is extremely difficult to cultivate because of its fragile roots. Specimens can, however, sometimes be purchased already grafted on to stronger stock. This Clianthus was first discovered by the explorer William Dampier when he voyaged to North Western Australia, which today is known as Dampier's Archipelago.

The Parrot Bill (*C. puniceus*) was first cultivated by the Maoris in New Zealand and although it still thrives naturally on North Island, it has already become extinct in many of its former territories.

Best grown in a hanging basket or any similar container where the trailing stems and blooms are displayed to the full, the Clianthus requires a constant temperature in the region of 60°F (15.5°C). Good even light is most important and so is careful watering, particularly in the autumn and winter. The compost — a standard houseplant mixture — must be quick draining, and the pot well-crocked with ample drainage holes. This helps to ensure that the roots never become waterlogged, which would really dash all your hopes of a blooming specimen.

# Coelogyne cristata

Orchids are generally considered very exotic and they are rather expensive because of their need for specialised treatment. These very slight and fragile creatures are mainly varieties which in the wild live on the ground. Many of the epiphytes — those which grow high up in the crevices of tree branches — are frequently easier to rear "in captivity". The only specialised housing they require is a cool to intermediate greenhouse.

Yet nowadays you can rear orchids indoors because there are several specimens which may be grown and displayed as delicate houseplants. And just think how exhilarated you will feel when you can honestly take the credit for rearing that ethereal-looking, softly-coloured orchid yourself!

One such species, which will produce anything up to eight pendant blooms in one go, is the Himalayan *Coelogyne cristata*. The three-inch long flowers are pure white except where they are broken at the lip with a gentle golden shading. The plants bloom in profusion from December to March and may prove even more prolific when growth is limited to an apparently over-small pot. Depending on the size of your specimen, this can vary from a three-inch to a five-inch container. Throughout the flowing period the compost must be kept just moist, no more, but unlike most of our more conventional indoor plants which bloom during the winter, this orchid should be watered very freely after the trailing blossoms have faded and the treatment should be continued through to October. Humidity, and lots of it, must surround it at all times (see pages 14–15), together with ample but draught-free fresh air, particularly in the warmer months.

**Coelogyne cristata**

Every other year the *Coelogyne cristata* will need a fresh mixture of two parts of finely-shredded osmunda fibre, one part of sphagnum moss and one part of sterilised leafmould (see page 17). This operation may be timed for the onset of spring and combined with the splitting up of the specimen to propagate new plants.

# Columnea

This multifarious tribe includes between 150 and 200 diffrent species, and these may be found growing from Mexico to Central America, Brazil and Bolivia. The red and yellow flowers secrete generous supplies of nectar, of which the humming-birds are particularly fond, and consequently these tiny creatures work as Nature's agents by pollinating the tubular heads as they hover between one flower and the next.

All Columneas are epiphytes — plants which attach themselves to trees although they do not derive any nutriment from their living support. They are not parasites and it is only their relatively small root growth which forces them to look for outside help. When it comes to maintaining these limited root plants in the home, particularly when they are confined to a pot, they frequently fail because their owners water them too often for their needs. It is understandable, for with their long, trailing stems one can easily believe that their liquid requirements are great. When not in bloom their compost should be kept on the dry side but they love plenty of moisture sprayed onto their foliage. If this chore is performed frequently, long tubular heads will quickly appear from the leaf-joints. They look really lovely when displayed indoors in a hanging basket but wherever they are grown, they require a light position out of the sun.

Both the container and compost are particularly important, for the pot, which must be porous, should not be too large — the Columneas are best kept pot-bound — and the compost blend needs to be of a quick-draining nature. A peat-based mixture, perhaps some peat-moss added to J.I.P. No. 3, is perfect.

**Columnea**

They are happiest in an all-the-year-round temperature of around 65°F (18°C). When the summer arrives three- to four-inch cuttings will take in a sandy compost within about three weeks but, as with so many hanging varieties, the best effects are achieved when several cuttings, five or six perhaps, have been planted together.

# Crossandra

The genus "Crossandra" comprises some fifty shrubs in all but there are really only two which concern us, the *C. nilotica* and the *C. undulata* (Firecracker Flower). The *C. nilotica* is found growing from Ghana to Kenya and Tanzania, at heights of between 3,000 and 7,000 feet. Its name — nilotica — meaning "from the Nile Valley", suggests that it might be somewhat of a nomad. The brownish-red flower spikes open in spring and summer and, like the flowers of most members of this family, they are generally fairly long-lasting, when grown in a greenhouse that is, but trying to rear them in the home is much more difficult although not impossible.

**Crossandra**

The second species, the "Firecracker Flower", is an inhabitant of India and in the wild reaches a healthy height of some three feet, yet in flowerpots only rarely do they reach such a size. The salmon-pink blooms appear almost any time from spring to autumn when cultivated under glass. However, wherever they are kept, in greenhouses, conservatories or homes, they must be assured a constantly damp atmosphere, see pages 14–15. In the flowering season the compost must remain wettish by means of frequent but small quantities of tepid water. Good, yet filtered light, in abundance is an equally pertinent consideration, especially for those specimens growing indoors. But do make sure that your well-lit window-sill does not turn out to be a draughty death-bed! Cut your specimen back once blooming is over and any shoots about three inches long will eagerly root in a mixture of peat and sand, with the help of some bottom heat of around 70°F (21°C).

Afterwards re-pot them in J.I.P. No. 2, but for more established plants use J.I.P. No. 3 with some extra peat. In the colder months only water them enough to prevent the "soil" becoming bone-dry. By March they probably will have shed some of their leaves but after a mild pruning they will quickly recover their green coats again.

# Dipladenia splendens

The slight difficulty with this plant lies in maintaining the necessary temperature of 60°F (15.5°C) in the winter and 70°F (21°C) in the warmer months, but if this can be done in either a heated home or greenhouse, the Dipladenia can be yours, blooms and all, and they really are quite spectacular! Large and pink and slightly perfumed, they do not last very long individually, but there is always an almost continuous stream of new buds at the ready to last throughout the summer.

A lightly shaded siting, together with frequent but weak feedings of liquid fertiliser, is the perfect diet for those specimens which are well-established. Daily syringing is absolutely essential, and for those growing in the home this could be a bit awkward but if you use the shower as I do, you will find it less messy and certainly more efficient. Being natural climbers, some form of support is a must and during this growing period they will consume a fair quantity of water. Let any excess liquid drain away and ensure this by providing a peaty growing mixture in a well-drained pot.

Growth tends naturally to die back later in the autumn, and despite the fact that regular manuring will help to keep it going, it is far kinder to let the plant have its rest and prune it right back to within a couple of inches of soil level. Then shoots will quickly reappear in the spring and, if there seems to be too many of them, take a few off and root any three- to four-inch "pieces" in a mixture of peat and sand.

**Dipladenia splendens**

Unlike the Brazilian beauty above, *Dipladenia boliviensis*, as its name suggests, is an inhabitant of Bolivia. The blooms of this variety are a lovely white, the two-inch tubular heads have yellow throats, and they delight us throughout the summer and autumn. Somewhat smaller than its relative, it can tolerate slightly lower temperatures and this could prove a godsend to those who have little success with the "splendens".

# Gardenia jasminoides

*Cape Jasmine*

The days when a gentleman would not be seen without a fresh Gardenia in his button-hole may be sadly lost to us forever, and the only hopes of a resurgence of such a charming custom lie in the hearts of the romantics and the eternal optimists. Fortunately, there are still many people who keep a Gardenia plant of their own.

Although frequently referred to as a jasmine, it is nothing of the sort. It takes its name from Dr. Alexander Garden, a Scot by birth and education, who first lived and practised as a physician in Charleston, South Carolina during the 1700s. The Gardenias, with their sweetly perfumed blooms, are not particularly difficult subjects to keep alive, and yet for them to thrive and look really lovely they do need careful and detailed attention.

**Gardenia jasminoides**

First found in China in 1763, these beauties require a

winter warmth of at least 55°F (13°C) — in summer this will automatically increase, yet should never exceed 75°F (24°C). Temperatures must remain as static as possible, otherwise they will lose their flowering buds, and the same thing will happen if you vary greatly the amount of water given, which should preferably be rainwater, so try to keep the compost just damp at all times. Quite a lot of moisture can be absorbed through the Gardenia's rich green leaves, and daily spraying of only the luxuriant greenery is very important, particularly when the air surrounding the plant is very dry (see pages 14–15). Remember, the Gardenia will not thank you for any water allowed to collect in the open flower heads, so your syringing will have to be very delicately applied if you do not want the white blooms to turn a muddy yellow!

A good, yet filtered light — especially for those kept in greenhouses — suits them, and a mixture of equal parts of well-rotted leafmould, rich loam and sand, or J.I.P. No. 3, with regular feeding during the late spring and summer, contains all the essential nutrients.

# Ixora coccinea

### *Flame of the Woods*

This flowering evergreen shrub can be seen growing quite naturally out of doors in the tropics and is in fact a native of India and the East Indies. Visitors to Holland will also see it, this time growing in pots, for over there it has been a very popular houseplant for some time.

In this country, Ixoras are considered somewhat "demanding", no doubt because of their need for relatively high temperatures and humidity. Until fairly recently, the average householder was hard put to it to provide really

**Ixora coccinea**

ideal conditions, unless he or she owned a heated green-house, but things are changing now more and more home-owners are installing central heating.

Anyone who admires the Hydrangea blooms, composed of many smaller flowers, will certainly fall in love with the one-inch heads of the "Flame of the Woods". Apart from being renowned for their beauty, they have a delightful perfume, and with their brilliant red faces it is easy to understand how they derived their flaming nickname! Another variety of the same species — this time from the Indian Ocean — *Ixora borbonica* — has white blooms and particularly lovely leaves, the bright red veins of which stand out on a light green background. Unfortunately, they are even more delicate than the first, but are a real challenge for the enthusiast!

Winter temperatures need to be in the region of 65°F (18°C) and the compost must be kept almost, but not quite, dust dry. All-the-year-round good and even light is essential, although a fierce summer sun must always be avoided. At this time the foliage will need even more spraying than usual, combined with a high humidity (see pages 14–15). After flowering has ceased, watering should be reduced and manuring discontinued for about six weeks but when they start to sprout again, feeding should be gradually reintroduced.

Gently prune and re-pot them in early spring, in either J.I.P. No. 2, or a mixture of equal parts of leafmould, coarse sand and peat. For sterilising such home blends turn to page 17.

# Medinilla magnifica

## *Rose Grape*

The Rose Grape is the only plant I can think of which can look very casual in a beautifully elegant way. The small reddish flowers are at first glance a little insignificant yet clothed as they are in large shell-pink bracts (coloured leaves), they take on an aristocratic appearance. The unusual flower-heads, which are supported on long stems, bow far down over the sides of their container. With a second-year specimen — first year plants certainly bloom, but nothing like so profusely — the effect is dazzling!

The Rose Grape is not particularly difficult, as long as it is given controlled warmth, and with central heating this should not prove impossible. However, enthusiasts with only coal or electric fires must, I am afraid, forget this variety. Ideal temperatures in the colder months are in the range of 65°F (18°C), but while they are blooming 70°F (21°F) is better — but a little variation either way will not harm them. You will certainly know if they approve of the general conditions, for a happy plant is a fast grower and will need only a comparatively short time

**Medinilla magnifica**

to reach a height of about four feet. A high humidity is the next most important point (see pages 14–15).

They come from the Philippines where they were discovered in 1888. They like a good but shaded light and a damp compost while producing leaves and flowers, but when they are resting you should not manure them and you should greatly reduce their water intake. Prune back any untidy growth and only when new growth is apparent should you give them a fresh mixture of sterilised leafmould, peat and sand. (For sterilising see page 17.)

# Pachystachys lutea

*Lollipop Plant*

This plant is often likened to the Zebra Plant (*Aphelandra*) but for those who have never seen the Lollipop I would describe the coloured bracts as being more akin to those of the Shrimp Plant (*Beloperone guttata*), except that these bracts are a lovely yellow and, as you can see from the

209

sketch, they stand erect like a well-licked lolly on a stick!

The Lollipop is particularly prone to white fly. These sap-sucking pests usually congregate on the undersides of leaves, which makes them more difficult to detect. However, if the little moth-like creatures are attacked immediately and persistently with a liquid Derris or Malathion spray (or any suitable houseplant pesticide) until all signs of them have disappeared, they should not present too much of a problem. Do not forget that a daily inspection is a wise precaution.

**Pachystachys lutea**

Lovers of warmth and bright light, the Lollipops require a temperature in the region of 60°F (15.5°C), but all this is well worth while just to enjoy the bracts and the white flowers which emerge any time from May until the late autumn. During this long blooming period they will need regular feeding and plenty of water but once growth begins to slow down, the liquid intake must be gradually reduced and finally stopped altogether until the spring.

Although this native of tropical South America is a perennial, it is sometimes better to grow it as an annual. Cuttings will root easily in a temperature of 70°F (21°C) in the spring and may be taken when you prune back your older specimens. Only use those pieces which look strong and healthy and keep the compost barely moist, otherwise the soft stems will quickly rot.

# CHAPTER
# FOURTEEN

# Flowering plants — temporary

## Achimenes

*Hot-water Plant*

The *Achimenes* makes a splendid pot plant, particularly for those who do not consider a plant worth having unless it produces lots of brightly-coloured blooms. Apart from the original violet-blue strain from Central America, there are now other colours such as white, mauve, blue, pink and red.

**Achimenes**

The small scaly tubers must be handled carefully when you plant them, which can be any time from February to May, but the earlier this is done the better. A six-inch pot will take six or seven tubers and these should be set about three-quarters of an inch deep. Your growing medium may be a standard potting compost such as J.I.P. No. 2, or a mixture of two parts of leafmould, two parts of peat, half a part of J.I.P. No. 2 and half a part of coarse sand. (For sterilising it see page 17.) Their first watering should be generous, but subsequent ones need to be given only sparingly until the growth is well-established. Indoors, they need a nice light spot near the window, but if you are growing them in a greenhouse, they will almost certainly need some shading. Keep the temperature as near 60°F (15.5°C) as you can.

Once flowering is over at the end of the summer the stems will die back naturally, and then both the pot and its occupants can be over-wintered in a cupboard until the following year. Remove the tubers in the early spring and, if necessary, divide them up before re-potting them in fresh compost. If, however, the mixture you used was particularly good, you need merely to soak the pot in luke-warm water before placing it in a fairly warm spot.

# Amaryllis belladonna

The Amaryllis belladonna, also known as the "Belladonna Lily", is a native of South Africa and there it may be seen growing wild along the coastline and near rivers and streams. Because of the sweet lingering fragrance of the flower-heads they attract many differing species of moths. Introduced into cultivation about 1712, the Amaryllis is often mistaken for another genus known as the Hippeastrum, but this latter variety may be found only in warmer climes. A single bulb may be set in a six-inch pot, to which has been added a layer of crocks and a piece of turf placed grass-side downwards. A suitable growing medium of either equal parts of J.I.P. No. 2, well-rotted manure and sand, or alternatively, two parts of J.I.P. No. 2 to one part of sand may be used, and it should be firmed down before the bulb is set at a depth of one-third of its height. More compost should then be added, so that the nose of the bulb is exposed just above the compost and just below the rim of the pot.

Ample water is needed immediately after planting but then refrain from giving more than a very little. Even that is best given "from below". Once the tall flower stems supporting the fragrant deep pink trumpet-shaped blooms are growing well, the quantity of liquid may be gradually increased. The flowers may appear any time between

**Amaryllis belladonna**

December and February and are quickly followed by a number of long strap-like leaves which may measure anything up to 30 inches in length. These leaves last throughout the winter months.

A low temperature of around 61°F (16°C) and a well-lit window-sill seem to suit them best. When the flowering period is over, all watering must cease and the potted bulbs should be removed to a cool, dry, frost-free garden room or shed. There they may remain until the following autumn.

# Azalea indica

## *Indian Azalea*

Practically all the Indian Azaleas offered for sale today are hybrids and many years of loving care have gone into producing the single or double flowers of white, pink, salmon, orange, crimson and magenta. They are both pleasant to the eye and well suited to indoor cultivation but the original species did not come from India, as one would suppose, but from China.

Another species of Azalea was discovered in the East Indies which was very similar to the *Azalea indica*, except for the flower formation, and one can only assume that it was because of this similarity that it eventually became known as the Indian Azalea.

Many thousands of Azaleas are given as presents every year but far too many die unnecessarily, so let us hope that this page may serve to prevent this. Correct watering is the main difficulty but in this case it is as if nature had anticipated such a problem by building in an instant moisture-meter, in the form of a ring water mark. When the ring is just above the compost level the plant is ready for a drink. If it is near the top the compost must be

**Azalea indica**

allowed to dry out or rotting may easily occur. Rain or soft tap-water should be used and to prolong the flowering period a well-lit room and a temperature not exceeding 55°F (13°C) is necessary.

All dead blooms must be carefully removed and to keep your plant from one year to the next prune it lightly before moving it into a cool light spot in the garden as soon as the possibility of frost has passed. If this is not possible, a balcony or unheated room will serve the same purpose if you plunge the pot into a hole or box containing peat. Even if it is out-of-doors it will still need frequent spraying of the foliage and compost until early autumn when it must return indoors.

# Begonia tuberhybrida

In the main, these tuberous Begonias are grown as pot plants but, whether indoors or displayed outside in tubs and garden borders, they always look magnificent!

Most of us have favourite colours and people who have

a special weakness for yellow blooms generally will surely love *B.t. Festiva* and the trailing strains Dawn and Golden Shower. The latter name alone sounds more like a dazzling firework than a brilliant hanging Begonia but the branches are indeed a shower of sheer gold. Some of the exquisite pinks include Rosanna and Rhapsody, whilst Rose Cascade will thrill you with its many arms, each full of rosy blooms flowing over the sides of the container. In fact all the Pendula strains are seen at their best when displayed in hanging baskets. My own favourites include the *B.t.* Seville (yellow and pink), the delicate orange heads of Mary Heatley, the white and pink Harlequin, the fluted yellow petals of Jamboree, which are tinged with orange — I really could go on and on!

**Begonia tuberhybrida**

The tubers are purchased around March when they should be set, hollow side upwards, in boxes of damp peat. With some warmth, say about 65°F (18°C), they will soon sprout to life. Transfer them to five-inch pots, and after a period of about a month and a half, a fertiliser may be fed to them every other week. Throughout the growing period the compost must be kept moist and the feeding continued until the end of the season. Keep your Begonias blooming in a draught-free siting, which affords them an unfluctuating 60°F (15.5°C).

Once the foliage starts to die, watering should be gradually reduced, and when the compost is completely dry the tubers can be lifted and rested in boxes of dry peat or sand at a temperature of about 45°F (7°C) — until the following year.

# Chrysanthemum

We all know the attractive indoor Chrysanthemums, which used to be associated with Christmastide, but now, with the aid of special techniques, they are available all the year round. They are not natural miniatures at all, but ordinary Chrysanthemums which have been specially treated with carefully regulated doses of dwarfing chemicals. Compact plants they may be indoors, but do not expect them to stay that way once flowering has ended and they are planted outside in the garden. Then they will have nothing to retard their normal growth, except perhaps a pruning which will keep them nice and bushy.

Chrysanthemums must be one of the oldest plants on record because as far back as 500 BC they were mentioned in the ancient horticultural books in China and the crossing of various colours during the T'ang dynasty produced many different cultivars, including the purple and white varieties. There was a belief that dew collected from the flower-heads would restore a man's vitality, and that eating the petals over a regular period would make the person concerned immortal.

A cool and well-lit spot will keep your Chrysanthemums

**Chrysanthemum**

at their best but remember that when the room is cosily warm for you, the flowers of most varieties will not stay fresh for very long. They will need watering, probably once a day, or when the top-soil starts to dry out. Keeping your eye on the compost is by far the best moisture guide, although Chrysanthemums are difficult plants to over-water anyway!

# Cineraria cruenta

The Cineraria is a native of the Canary Islands and, though a half-hardy perennial, it is usually cultivated in greenhouses and conservatories as a biennial. This variety produces an abundance of richly-coloured blooms, ranging in colour from white to lilac, blue, pink, mauve and red, and there is also a wide selection of flowering two-toned types as well.

Seeds are sown thinly in trays of seed compost any time from April to August and the resulting plants bear blooms

**Cineraria cruenta**

during the winter and through to the following spring. The seeds need a germinating temperature of 55°F (13°C) and when the seedlings are large enough to handle they are pricked out and potted singly into three-inch pots containing J.I.P. No. 1 compost. If they are to grow strong and bushy, care must be taken to give them a very light position, but in the summer months one must provide some protection from the burning rays of the sun. As the fast-growing plants out-grow their containers, they should be "potted on" into one-size larger pots containing four parts of J.I.P. No. 2 and one part of sand. Their final potting should be in one of six- or seven-inches. Once the flower buds develop they should be fed every ten to fourteen days with a good houseplant fertiliser and a fairly cool temperature of around 61°F (16°C) should be maintained.

The moist compost must never become soggy or, almost inevitably, this will lead to "grey mould", "collar" or "root rot", all of which may occur when the cultural conditions are excessively cool and wet. Winter-flowering specimens need as much light as possible and those growing in the home will bloom more readily on a southerly- or westerly-facing window-sill, where they may obtain the maximum amount of natural light.

# Cyclamen persicum

*Cyclamen, Sowbread*

I love the Cyclamens because their delicate blooms and heart-shaped foliage are beautiful to look at, but the pig-farmers of Italy and France might not agree with me — they have more practical ideas on the subject. They use the corms of this Syrian and Mediterranean plant as food for their pigs! A waste perhaps, yet the locals, particularly in Périgord, claim that this somewhat unusual diet gives the pork a special and rather delicate flavour. Hence the plant is sometimes referred to as the Sowbread. Although I adore the taste of pork, I have yet to sample this treated delicacy but, rather than risk a shortage of flowering Cyclamens in the future, I prefer to continue eating the less original plain roast pork!

The original variety, which was first discovered in 1731, had small white or pink blooms and was deliciously fragrant. Over the years some of the original perfume has been re-introduced into the now much larger pastel-coloured flowers but we are still no further forward in producing the scent in the more brilliant shades of red.

The Cyclamen is often purchased around Christmas time to add colour to our often flowerless living-rooms. It requires plenty of light and any sun at this time of the year will not harm it. A steady warmth of about 60°F (15.5°C), with some fresh air without draughts, will keep it happy. Provide it with a moist atmosphere and it will rejoice but, as you will see on pages 14–15, this does not mean a soggy compost! Neither is a dry compost advised but something in between. To maintain such a delicate liquid balance frequent waterings, giving only small amounts at a time, are the answer.

**Cyclamen persicum**

# Erica

## *Heathers*

The moors of Scotland are invigorating and yet so peaceful, the stillness being broken only by the occasional plaintive cry of the curlew and the whirring sound of the rising grouse. But it is the bed of heather stretching for miles, like some never-ending blanket, which really catches the eye. Growing wild and unaided, it is richly coloured, springy and robust, but when man lends a "helping" hand, it seems to cringe and often curls up and dies!

The cultivated Erica originates in South Africa. This tiny plant can look exquisite when given the chance. A good start is to transfer new arrivals with tightly matted roots into a slightly larger pot, firming them in position with some moistened peat and sharp sand. Then water them well, using very slightly warmed soft tap- or rain-water. Because they are lime-haters, no trace of chalk should be present in the water they drink or the compost in which they live, otherwise they they will turn yellow and fail miserably. Whenever the top-soil begins to look dry, immerse the entire pot in water and wait until all the air bubbles have stopped. Only then can you be sure that it is evenly moistened throughout.

**Erica**

Keep your heathers in a cool and light environment where the air is inclined to be on the damp side (see pages 14–15).

At the beginning of April, cut the shoots back to a tidier

shape, thereby encouraging a more free-branching growth and, when all signs of frost are past, put them outside in a sheltered spot. There they may remain until late August or early September, but during this time make sure that they do not have to rely entirely on the rain. Check them every day.

# Euphorbia pulcherrima

*Poinsettia, Christmas Star*

The Poinsettia has for some time been a very great favourite as a traditional Christmas gift in Europe and the United States. It is not, as is generally believed, the flowers which make it so popular but the coloured leaves (bracts) of cream, pink or red which frame the insignificant little yellow blooms.

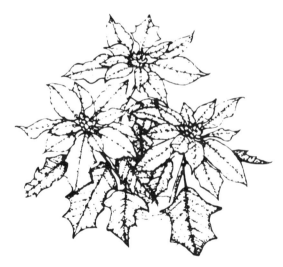

**Euphorbia pulcherrima**

They were introduced into Europe about 1830, from their native tropical Mexico, where they reach tree-like proportions. They rarely exceed five feet when cultivated,

224

because the nurseryman treats them with carefully regulated doses of dwarfing chemicals, which keep them to a saleable size. If you keep your plant from one year to the next, you will really see it hit the heights, and after several years the ceiling will not necessarily be its limit! But not many people keep them after the first year because the complicated business of developing the coloured bracts involves both the curtailing and extension of daylight hours, under very controlled conditions, and in the majority of homes this is not practical.

Once the bracts and green leaves die and you decide to keep it, prune the stem back to within six inches of the J.I.P. No. 3 compost. Keep the soil dry and free from fertilisers until new shoots appear, then resume the watering. Re-pot it at this stage and from September onwards regular manuring is a good thing.

# Fuchsia

Isn't it odd how some people can be so contrary, just for the pure joy of it, when in the end it hurts no-one but themselves? Last summer, a lady, whom I know only slightly, asked me about a Fuchsia which had been given to her recently as a birthday present. I always avoid proffering advice unasked but, if invited, I am always happy to help, so I certainly was not forcing unwanted suggestions on her when I said that her potted specimen, which was a mass of tight buds, should be given a bright and sunny spot away from draughts.

A couple of weeks later I was again stopped by the same, now despondent, lady, who said that the Fuchsia flowers had all fallen whilst still in bud. I went with her to her home and found that she had been keeping it in an extremely dark and draughty hallway! Apparently she had decided that there was where *she* wanted it to be, not for one moment considering what the plant wanted!

**Fuchsia**

Fuchsias are never the easiest plants to keep in the home but if you can keep them in a greenhouse or conservatory they are the simplest and most rewarding of flora. Indoors, a new arrival will sometimes shed its flowers and foliage if there is a sudden change in conditions. Then it is best to remove all the buds so that the plant can recover more quickly from its shock! No such problems should arise if it is kept in a cool room of approximately 50°F (10°C), has ample fresh air, a moist atmosphere (see pages 14–15) and careful watering.

Let your J.I.P. No. 3 compost become almost dry in between summer waterings and, in the winter, limit its drinking habits to perhaps one a month — and keep it cool!

# Solanum capsicastrum

*Winter Cherry, Christmas Cherry*

The Solanum, often called the Winter, or Christmas Cherry, is a flowering pot plant but in this case the star-shaped flowers are of little interest; it is the miniature orange-like fruits, which form after the blooms have died, which make this little Brazilian such a gem!

They are classified as temporary plants because they are nearly always discarded once the berries have fallen but they can be kept for another year. About March of the second season one third of the growth should be pruned, before re-potting them in a slightly larger container with J.I.P. No. 2.

**Solanum capsicastrum**

New plants may be propagated in two ways, and once you have purchased your first, there is no reason why you cannot have a fresh supply every year! If you have keen green fingers you can sow the seeds contained in the fruit in seed compost, and in a temperature of 65°F (18°C) seedlings will quickly appear. As soon as they are big enough to handle, re-pot them separately in J.I.P. No. 2. Alternatively, three-inch side-shoots will also root in equal parts of peat and coarse sand round about July and, once rooted, can be re-planted in the J.I.P. mixture.

Over-winter them in a frost-free greenhouse and by May some can be used to decorate window-boxes outside, while the rest of them may be ensconced indoors. Provide your plant with the conditions it likes — a winter temperature of at least 50°F (10°C), a damp to moist compost throughout, and lots of bright light and it will retain its pleasing appearance.

# Tulips

The word "tulip" is derived from the Turkish word "tulbend", meaning turban, and this apt description refers to the brilliant blooms which closely resemble the colourful draped headgear of the Turks. The first known tulip, *Tulipa gesneriana*, was named after Conrad Gesner, who discovered it in Constantinople and brought it to Augsburg during the mid-sixteenth century. "Prepared" bulbs are first stored in a cold place to encourage early growth and are suitable for early flowering in the home.

Early single varieties suitable for pot culture are "Apricot Beauty", with apricot-coloured heads supported on fifteen inch (37.5cm) tall flower stems, and the sweetly-perfumed golden flowering "Bellona". Three slightly lower-growing strains of around twelve inches are "Mon Trésor", which has perfumed heads of golden yellow, "Brilliant Star", a popular indoor bulb which produces brilliant scarlet orange heads, and the scarlet and sweetly-perfumed "Vermilion Brilliant". Others are the orange scarlet blooms of "Prince of Austria", the violet-flowering "Van der Neer", "Peter Pan", with pink and cream heads, and one of the best of all tulips for forcing, the "Christmas Marvel" which bears bright cherry-coloured flowers.

Pots or bowls may be filled with either specially prepared bulb-fibre or a mixture consisting of two parts J.I.P. No. 2, one part of peat and one part of sand. The latter growing medium is by far the best because, unlike bulb-fibre, it contains nutrients to feed the growing bulbs. Tulips are delicate and inclined to bruise easily, so when it comes to planting them, handle them with extreme care. Always set them so that their noses are below the rim of the container, and just covered with compost. Water them lightly before taking them out into the garden and covering them with a six inch layer of sand. Alternatively, the bowls may be wrapped in black polythene and placed inside a very cool and dark cupboard.

**Tulip**

When provided with too much warmth and light tulips are inclined to go blind. So it is important to leave them until they have grown about four inches before they are ready to be brought into a cool and moderately light room. Gradually acclimatise them to warmer and brighter conditions but do so very slowly or they will fail. The compost must be kept nicely moist at all times.

# Veltheimia viridifolia

## Syn. V. capensis

The Veltheimia viridifolia (*Syn. V. capensis*), a member of the Lily family, is better known as the "Forest Lily". A native of Cape Province, it was discovered more than two hundred years ago by Linnaeus, and was eventually named after the great eighteenth-century patron of botany, Count Veltheim. The oval-shaped bulbs may be planted any time between August and September and, being fairly large,

**Veltheimia viridifolia**

even a single bulb needs plenty of space. It is best set at a depth of two-thirds of its height in a five-inch pot containing a mixture of equal parts of either well-rotted manure, peat and J.I.P. No. 2, or decomposed leafmould and J.I.P. No. 2.

It is most important that these bulbs are given an extremely cool room of around 45°F (7°C), especially for the first three or four weeks of their growing life. They should never be subjected to great heat at any time, and a sunless position on any but a southerly-facing window-sill suits them very well. The Forest Lily must not be watered too freely at first or it will rot. Feed it just sufficient liquid to encourage rooting and only when the dark green strap-like leaves are growing well may the quantity of water be slowly increased, but always avoid splashing the foliage. The tall twelve inch (30cm) flower stems support an inflorescence comprising many tubular-like pinkish blooms, dotted with yellow, and these beautiful heads appear any time between December and April. When blooming the compost should be watered only when it appears almost dry, and once flowering ceases, watering must be discontinued.

The bulbs may be dried off by placing them, with their pots, on their sides in a very sunny spot. This will encourage them to ripen. The following autumn they should be started into growth in the same pot. In the second year, after the blooming period has ended, the bulbs should be carefully lifted and the offsets attached to the parent bulb separated and set in small pots containing equal parts of J.I.P. No. 1 and sand. After tending them in the usual way for two years, these young bulbs may be grown on in the mixture suggested for mature bulbs and, within a year or two, they will begin to flower.

# Index

232

# INDEX

Nerve Plant, 114
Nicotine spray, 20
*Nolina recurvata*, 62
Norfolk Islands Pine, 87

Offsets, 25
Old Man's Beard, 184
Oleander, 168
Opuntia, 2
Over-watering, 4, 7, 21, 22

*Pachystachys lutea*, 209
Painted Nettle, 44
Painter's Palette, 25, 191
*Pandanus*, 66
Parlour Palm, 91, 98
Parrot Bill, 196
*Passiflora caerulea*, 170
Passion Flower, 170
Peacock Plant, 97
Peat, 15, 27, 28
*Pellionia*, 119
*Peperomia*, 121
  *sandersii*, 28
Pests, 19, 20
*Philodendron bipinnatifidum*,
  122
  *leichtinii*, 124
  *panduraeforme*, 67
  *scandens*, 3, 125
Phoenix dactylifera, 127
Pickaback Plant, 6, 7, 139
Piggyback Plant, 139
*Pilea*, 29, 69
Pineapple, 35

*Piper nigrum*, 70
  *ornatum*, 70
Pistol Plant, 70
*Platycerium bifuratum*, 129
*Pleomele reflexa variegata*, 72
Poinsettia, 224
Polythene, 10, 24, 27, 28, 30
Pony Tail, 63
Prayer Plant, 25, 114
Pricking out, 24
Primulas, 3
Propagating, 22 *et seq.*
Purple Heart, 28

Rabbits' Tracks, 14, 114
Rain, 7
Red-Hot Cat's Tail, 190
Red spider, 20
*Regal pelargoniums*, 172
*Rex Begonia*, 27, 36
Rhizomes, 115
*Rhoicissus rhomboidea*, 2, 130
Rice Paper Plant, 77
Root rot, 15, 21, 52
Rooting powder, hormone, 29,
  30
*Rosa chinensis minima*, 174
Rosary Vine, 40
Rose Bay, 168
  Grape, 208
  of China, 161
  Mallow, 161
Rubber Plant, 2, 3, 5, 29, 30, 32
  Indian, 55
Runners, 25, 27

PUBLISHER'S NOTE

# John Innes Composts

These were developed by the John Innes Horticultural Institution for its own use in research. The Institution published the formulae to allow others to make use of it.

## JOHN INNES POTTING COMPOST NO. 1
   7 parts loam (partially sterilized)
   3 parts peat (fibrous or granulated)  parts by
   2 parts sand (washed  volume
      horticultural)

To each bushel (36 litres) of the mixture add:
   113g (4oz/8 tblspoons) base fertiliser consisting of
      2 parts hoof and horn meal
      2 parts superphosphate of lime
      1 part sulphate of potash
   21g (¾oz/1½ tblspoons) ground chalk

## JOHN INNES POTTING COMPOST NO. 2
To each bushel (36 litres) of the mixture add twice the amount of fertilizer and chalk.

## JOHN INNES POTTING COMPOST NO. 3
To each bushel (36 litres) of the mixture add three times the amount of fertilizer and chalk.

## JOHN INNES SEED COMPOST

2 parts loam (partially sterilized)  
1 part medium peat  
1 part sand  
} parts by volume

To each bushel (36 litres) of the mixture add:

42g (1½oz/3 tblspoons) superphosphate of lime  
21g (¾oz/1½ tblspoons) ground chalk

## CUTTING COMPOST

For rooting cuttings, use a mixture of 50% peat and 50% sand only.

# ISIS
large print books

We hope that you have enjoyed this book and will want to read more.

We list some other titles on the next few pages. All our books may be purchased from ISIS at either of the addresses below.

If you are not already a customer, or on our mailing list, please write and ask to be put on the mailing list for regular information about new ISIS titles.

We would also be pleased to receive your suggestions for titles that you would like us to publish in large print. We will look into any suggestions that you send to us.

Happy reading.

**ISIS, 55 St Thomas' Street, Oxford OX1 1JG, ENGLAND, tel (0865) 250333**

**ISIS, ABC – CLIO, 2040 Alameda Padre Serra, PO Box 4397, Santa Barbara, CA 93140 – 4397, USA**

# ALSO AVAILABLE IN LARGE PRINT

**Longman English Dictionary**
**Longman Medical Dictionary**
**Longman Thesaurus**
**Hammond Large Type World Atlas**

| | |
|---|---|
| Letts Retirement Guides | **Finance** |
| Letts Retirement Guides | **Good Health** |
| Letts Retirement Guides | **House and Garden** |
| Letts Retirement Guides | **Leisure and Travel** |
| Robert Dougall | **Years Ahead** |
| Margaret Ford | **'In Touch' at Home** |
| Consumers Association | **Dealing with Household Emergencies** |
| Moyra Bremner | **Supertips to Make Life Easy** |
| Rabbi Lionel Blue | **Kitchen Blues** |
| William R Hartston | **Teach Yourself Chess** |
| Kenneth Beckett | **The Love of Gardening** |
| Desmond Morris | **Catwatching** |
| Desmond Morris | **Dogwatching** |
| Andrew Young | **A Prospect of Flowers** |
| Leon Garfield | **Shakespeare Stories** |
| Lord Birkenhead (Editor) | **John Betjeman's Early Poems** |
| Joan Duce | **I Remember, I Remember . . .** |
| Dan Sutherland | **Six Miniatures** |
| Beryl Reid | **The Cat's Whiskers** |